A Life of Thoughts

Selections from the Writings of Chittaranjan Das

A Life of Thoughts

Selections from the Writings of Chittaranjan Das

Edited By

Sampad Patnaik

Jatindra Kumar Nayak

BLACK EAGLE BOOKS
Dublin, USA | Bhubaneswar, India

Black Eagle Books
USA address:
7464 Wisdom Lane
Dublin, OH 43016

India address:
E/312, Trident Galaxy, Kalinga Nagar,
Bhubaneswar-751003, Odisha, India

E-mail: info@blackeaglebooks.org
Website: www.blackeaglebooks.org

First International Edition Published by
Black Eagle Books, 2024

A LIFE OF THOUGHTS
Selections from the Writings of Chittaranjan Das

Edited by **Sampad Patnaik**
Jatindra Kumar Nayak

Cover & Interior Design: Ezy's Publication

ISBN- 978-1-64560-541-6 (Paperback)
Library of Congress Control Number: 2024935384

Printed in the United States of America

Acknowledgements

We thank the members of the Chittaranjan Das Centenary Committee, and acknowledge our deep indebtedness to its Chairperson Sri Soumya Ranjan Patnaik and Convenor Sri Bharat Bhusan Mohanty. We convey our thanks to Sri Anil Pradhan, Member Secretary of Sikshasandhan for his enthusiastic support and cooperation. We express our warm appreciation to Dr Shaswat Panda for copyediting the manuscript meticulously. We thank Asis Nanda and Naba Ho for their support from Sikshasandhan Library. We are grateful to Mr. Satya Pattanaik of Black Eagle Books for publishing this collection. We express sincere thanks to the translators, who devoted their precious time making the writings of Das accessible to readers outside Odisha.

Introduction

The volume presents a selection from the translated writtings of Chittaranjan Das (1923-2011). These essays introduce the reader to an extraordinary adventure in the realm of ideas and an exceptional human being who ceaselessly experimented with new ways of experiencing the world and of thinking about it.

Born in 1923 in a village in undivided Cuttack district, Das received his early education at Ranihat High School and Ravenshaw Collegiate School. While a student at Ravenshaw College, Das gave up his studies to plunge into the Quit India movement led by Mahatma Gandhi. He was arrested and jailed by the British authorities. A remarkable and exciting intellectual journey began after he was released from jail, which continued till the very end of his life.

Das studied at Santiniketan and soon after Independence spent several years at Denmark, closely studying an institution called Folk School. Returning to India, he joined a school set up in a forest in Angul and conducted pedagogic experiments which he has memorably recorded in two volumes--- *Jibana Bidyalaya* (The School of Life) and *Jungle Chithi* (Letters from the Jungle).

Das briefly taught sociology at Agra University after

leaving this school. He remained a restless wanderer who travelled to every nook and corner of Odisha, many parts of India, and countries, such as Nepal, Germany, Israel, and America.

Thereafter, Das dedicated himself to a life devoted to reading, writing, translating, publishing books, and engaging in innovative educational initiatives. Although he had abandoned institutions dispensing formal education, Das remained a passionate seeker and disseminator of knowledge all his life. More than 200 books he published include an autobiography, translations, literary histories, biographies, treatises, diaries, collections of letters, books for children, and travelogues. However, the essay remained his favoured medium of self-expression and instrument of intervention.

The essay, which took shape in the rapidly changing world of 19th Century Odisha under the influence of western literary sensibilities, perfectly suited Das' iconoclastic and interrogative outlook on history, culture, and society. In essay after essay, with a dazzling array of themes, he not only sought to expand the frontiers of knowledge but also to shake the reader out of ethical and intellectual complacency. Das relentlessly prodded the reader to question ossified beliefs and entrenched conventions and instead embrace tolerant and cosmopolitan attitudes.

A polyglot, Das introduced Odia readers to the diversity of intellectual traditions, represented by figures such as Spinoza, Martin Buber, Gandhi, Aurobindo, and Vivekananda. Das' impatience with received notions and passive prejudices often drew him to deploy the resources of incisive irony and mordant satire in many of his essays. For instance, in the essay titled "The Omnipresent Babus,"

Das presents a searing critique of the bureaucracy, a startling departure from the uncritical adoration most educated Odias reserve for the profession.

This trait in Das sometimes led many to portray him as a cynic. However, the label utterly misrepresents the mission his essays sought to fulfil. His sarcasm, irony, and anger emanated essentially from a wellspring of profound concern for humanity. These he used as a weapon to attack hypocrisy, intellectual chicanery, and stagnation of the mind.

Das was no ivory tower intellectual. These essays were not written in splendid isolation. They were informed by an intimate experience of the street, village, and forest, away from professional thinkers, such as academics and other salaried classes. The best example of this is the essay "Seven Days in the Ganjam Highlands". The essays dispensed a kind of knowledge that is not to be found in academic dissertations and treatises.

Das' approach to knowledge and experience was remarkable for its refusal to sentimentalize any way of life. He was willing to subject the familiar and the unique to equal, withering scrutiny. In the essay "To Which Gods?", Das indicts European literature for allowing itself to be intoxicated by power and glorifying nationalism and imperialism, which led to great human suffering across the world.

However, Das' rebellious instinct was tempered by a deep and abiding compassion for fellow human beings and a faith in the intrinsic nobility of the ordinary. He has written with great emotion about the suffering of tribals, who we have trained to become "tamed elephants" that will "dance in our streets". In "A Portrait of Tribal Culture", Das writes: The real growth and development of tribal people is possible only by tribal leadership, never by feudal lords. The day on which a tribal can speak on his own about his culture and its past and future, a truthful description of the tribals will be available.

Das passionately invested himself in the essay as a literary form. No wonder, he authored an entire book titled *Prabandha ra Pruthibi* (The World of the Essay). In his view, the importance of the essay lies in its resistance to the idea that literature is a source of amusement and consolation. Das defines the essay in terms of the seriousness of its purpose — its aim is to use richly nuanced prose to celebrate the "examined life". The significance of the essay stems from its role as a "midwife" that facilitates the birth of consciousness.

We sincerely hope this selection of essays illustrates the diverse strands of ethical thoughts that Das wove into his writings over a lifetime.

SAMPAD PATNAIK

JATINDRA KUMAR NAYAK

Table of Contents

Seven Days in the Highlands of Ganjam

The Madras Mail reached Berhampur before the crack of dawn. We could not know when, in the darkness, we had crossed the Chilika coast. I made my way out of the crowded compartment and on to the station platform. I had not slept well. My face was swollen like that of a sullen boy. With coal dust getting into my eyes, I dusted myself and moved towards the town.

If Cuttack is famous for its rickshaws, Berhampur is famous for its pulled rickshaws. These pulled rickshaws are ubiquitous across small and big towns in Southern India.

The pulled rickshaws are mostly handled by Telugu speaking people. Young Telugu chaps from Visakhapatnam have come to dominate the roads of Cuttack. I read it in history books that the kings from the South had founded the Ganga dynasty in Odisha; the Telugu king Mukundadev had integrated the culture by conquering the North and the South. But these days men are hired differently. Migration is caused by starvation. I do not know if the human contractors of Visakhapatnam really solve the issue of starvation, as I do not know where the paddy and ragi cultivated in the middle eastern coastal belt go. But there must be some reason for a young Telugu boy to come to Cuttack to pull a rickshaw, and to be one among the able rickshaw-pullers of Pattapur and Godisahi.

I hurried towards the middle part of the town. As the sun rose, the garbage strewn across the city was becoming prominently visible. People were going about their business amidst the shops, bazaar, dust, leaves, and some begging naked children. Adding to the chaos, were some stray bullocks and cows. Of course, I have not kept account of the sight of streets of the U.S. and the U.K.

I did not know which bus to take to Udayagiri. After receiving some guidance from folks at the bus stand, I boarded a bus that was carrying iron rods. By the time the bus had left, it was past eight in the morning. The bus began to move slowly, leaving behind the plains near the seashore. The view of most villages from both sides of the bus was indistinct from each other: houses, cowsheds, groves of mango and jackfruit, and the barren fields post-harvest. It was the same sights one might encounter from the foothills of the Himalayas to Kanyakumari.

We passed through Digapahandi, also known as Badakhemundi. Then the hilly regions came up. The engine of our bus started groaning as it went up the steep road. Suddenly, I could hear the burbling sound of the hot water spring that lay ahead. I had read about this hot water spring in a travelogue. Our bus stopped by the spring. Some of us went up to have a darshan of the resident Goddess Taptapani, while some preferred to take a dip in its waters.

Taptapani is a famous hot water spring in Ganjam district. The hot water has been gushing out of a particular spot for centuries. The government or some generous person has built a wall around it. There were some stones in the water; some small stones were smeared with sindoor. Wherever humans have come across something uncommon, they have placed flowers and sindoor and woven mysteries around the place.

Taptapani is quite sombre. Surrounded by hills and dense forest, this beautiful spot attracts many tourists. So many people from so many villages have kept this place vibrant. They believe water from this spring, if used in irrigation, will keep away insects that destroy crops. Perhaps, this belief explains the sight of farmers from distant places carrying water from this spring in vessels made from bamboo. In the past, whenever people have faced any obstacle, such faith has shown them a simple way out.

Leaving Taptapani behind, our bus kept going up the hills. It was noon. No one remembers where the iron rods fell from the bus. But the place where the vehicle dropped us had no inhabitants. The road forked at that point. I got to know from my co-passengers that Ramagiri-Udayagiri was thirty-two miles away, a distance that could be covered by two days of walking. Others said the distance was about five miles, or at best fifteen. Whatever the distance, 32 miles or 62 miles, we had to cover it.

We were in the middle of the jungle—on the right side was Mohana and on the left, Udaygiri. I began walking towards my destination. The baggage was light. In one hand, there was a leather suitcase, and, in the other, a leather sling bag. I began my journey at around one in the afternoon, gathering all my strength and eagerness.

The sky, too, seemed to walk with us. The clouds were dark, like the coating on pots by the hearth. The trees seemed to be conversing with one another. One could hear faint whistling.

I had come to Ganjam seven years ago. I had not yet forgotten the experience of travelling by bullock cart. This journey, after seven years of education, seemed new.

When the rains come over the mountains, the music of its blowing sound can be heard from long distances. Breaking the silent emptiness, the rains come with the speed of a comet. Reminded of that sound under a cloudy sky, I was startled.

Yes, it was going to rain. There is no habitation in sight. Where could I take shelter? Despite my soaked clothes, I trudged on. But I could not continue walking for long. I had to take shelter somewhere.

Someone from the same bus was coming along with me. His village was somewhere ahead. We had already covered almost two miles and had exchanged a few words. The man declared that he would be happy if I took rest on his veranda till the rains let up. My mind was restless. His offer seemed like an act of God. I agreed for there was no room for formality. My cowardice would not permit me to say no.

The village Sankulipada was a call away from the road. The village was very small, with rows of a few houses in a red earth coating. I had come across such houses in Banki and had liked them. Art is in the jungle, within our soil. For the poor, his walls, verandas, and deities are the canvas; his tools are the soil and cow dung, his fingers are his paintbrushes.

As soon as we reached the village, it started pouring. It seemed as if apprehending rain someone had arranged for shelter. The small houses had verandas with uneven width, where ragi was spread to dry.

That day I took shelter in that small village to protect myself from the rain. I was given water to wash my feet. I was asked to seat myself on a date palm mat that was unrolled on one corner of the veranda. I looked up to see when the sky was going to be clear so that I could move. At that time, tea was brought in from the front room. I received affection on the small veranda of a hut in a hamlet. Only in small villages, where there are no hotels, no offices, no issues of untimeliness, could one relate with another heart. Only a housewife in such a village could be like my mother, knowing exactly what I wanted.

While I was sipping tea, I was served with baked maize. All the gentlemanliness and sophistication I had acquired in my life disappeared that day, as I went on munching on the maize like a child. My ancestors were poor; they ate rice only during feasts. Mostly, they managed with ragi and kangu rice. All the villagers, likewise, were poor; no one's verandah was pucca and no one's thatch was at a height.

Around three in the afternoon, the sky cleared; the sound from the mountains ceased—the rain drifted away. But I had to go a long way. Breaking the emotional attachment that I was forming with the place—I had already ordered for a dinner of Kangu rice—I started my journey. My duty-bound, alert mind would not let me rest.

"After completing his study, Babu will come to our district as a high-ranking officer", I heard an old man of the house saying as I was coming out. Not quite unnatural. I live in Cuttack, study English on the other side of Calcutta. What would I become if not an officer?

"You are still studying, instead of getting married?" said a woman. Perhaps it was the same woman who had shown her hospitality by offering me baked maize and tea. The old man commented "Once he secures a job, will he not get four times the money that is now being spent on his education?"

I came out on to the road. All alone. With a sling bag and a suitcase, I walked straight through the same jungle, the same hills. I guessed the time by looking at the sun. My mind imagined many things as I walked through the green, wet land bathed in sunshine.

That was a market day in Chandipur. But by the time I reached there, the hawking and trading had ended. Here the markets begin in the morning and wind up by the afternoon. People return to their villages through the passages between the hills. Sending their crops to Brahmapur, they get a week's supply of salt, chillies, and sun-dried fish. Here, in the market place the village converges with the town.

Chandragiri, my scheduled stop for the night, was at eight miles away. I kept walking on my own. Sometimes I ran into people. I had brief conversations with them. I was introduced to many aspects of their lives, in which the heart was filled with affection and simplicity, the body endowed with strength, and the face marked by poverty.

It was twilight when I reached Chandragiri. The house in the middle of the village, with white-washed walls and high pillars, belonged to Mr Patra. He was like a Karana karji of big settlements. Collecting dues from the area, they deposit a portion with the King of Badakhemundi. The Panas and Sabaras of different villages have been assigned jagirs so that they would transport the goods of the government officers.

A pair of bullocks were tied near Patra's high veranda. He is the only rich man in the village, as though Goddess Lakshmi made him her vehicle while rendering thousands penniless.

Patra asked some people to accompany me to the bungalow and arranged for my food. Although the bungalow was small, it was quite neat and clean. The high-roofed thatched house of two rooms only had a cot, a table, and a chair. An inspector from the department of agriculture was staying in that house the same day. He facilitated my stay. I went to bed early, eating from the dishes cooked for him. While smelling the bed, I fell asleep.

I was awakened at dawn by the cawing of the first crow. Udayagiri lay ahead of the other half of the way. I quickly completed my morning chores and set out before the sun was up.

The path snaked through the dense jungle. I had the information that there were elephants in this jungle. But that day I did not come across any animals, except several young pythons. Wet from the previous night's rain, they lay inert on the road. The sun was yet to dry them.

I lack the words to describe my feelings while travelling alone through the jungle. I followed the path all alone, amidst the dense green leaves. My thighs were becoming weak after going up and down the terrain. Sometimes the hills would appear in my line of sight, but then the tall trees blocked my view. The absentminded man within me had turned me into the lone traveller Livingstone in the African jungles. Our circumstances maybe different but our experiences were the same. My solitary travel was in no way less than that of Livingstone. My mind travelled to Columbus, four and a half centuries ago.

Despite an empty stomach, I marched ahead. I had covered a long distance. The sun gradually rose from behind the hills. Hunger was gnawing at my stomach. There was no hamlet in sight. After walking around three kilometres, I reached a village called Mahendragada. I grew hopeful of getting food. I asked someone going towards the village if I could get to eat anything. He gave a blunt no, saying there was not a single eatery in the village. He gave me the hope that if I kept on walking I would reach the village Chheligada where all kinds of food would be available. Even though my hunger was unbearable, I continued to walk for three more kilometres. On the way I crossed Tirasua river. I reached Chheligada by nine that morning.

I was famished. Two boys led me to a shop. A poor householder had opened a minimal shop. It sold all sorts of things like chilli, cumin, bidi and cigarette. The only thing edible among them was fried rice and molasses. I had no option but to buy them. When I put some fried rice into my mouth I realised my throat was dry. From my parched throat came out the earnest question, "Isn't tea available here?"

Of all the people gathered there to watch me, an old man came out of the crowd and said, "It will be available in the next village." Taking a pause, he asked me if I would like to take tea from his house as he is a Christian.

No believer in the caste system to begin with, and with mounting hunger, I immediately said yes. The old man took me with him to his house. A mat made of hard reed was spread on the floor of a room. The lady in the house was cooking something like pan cake, made from ground rice. First came that, followed by tea. Acknowledging their hospitality, I drank three glasses of tea.

I was ready to resume my journey. Udaygiri was only four miles away. It was around 10 A.M. The clouds were accumulating over the Champa Ghat. Within a short span, the inhabitants of the Christian settlement of Chheligada had won over my heart. They were not willing to let me go alone. They insisted that one of them must accompany me. But they were in a crisis as it was a Sunday, and no one could move out until unless the Sunday service was over. Everyone agreed I should stay back for a few more hours.

One loves to stay at a place where one finds himself being loved. The love of the stranger-friends held me back. Changing my clothes, I followed them to the church.

The church was not like that of Cuttack, pointed and tall. This was a small, thatched house, constructed by the people collecting housing material from the jungle. The bell tolled every Sunday morning. The men, working regularly with the mud and soil, cleaned themselves once a week to attend the church services. They forgot all their worries in a moment of surrender. Into this mud house came God for a moment, for a moment the men were at peace.

The men and women were seated separately on either side of the aisle. I liked this practice of mass prayer in Christianity. Bringing together men with all kinds of nature under one umbrella, this religion was declaring the inner unity of human being. Forgetting the worries of mundane life, people get peace by coming together.

People of all ages, from the young to the old, gathered there. Date palm leaf mats were laid out for the congregation to sit. A broken chair and a table were placed up front. On the table was a cross, made by joining two split pieces of wood. The image of the great soul, who sacrificed his life making the misery of the poor people his own, is now on a bead of necklace around the necks of all the believers. He occupies the most important spot even in a broken shed in Chheligada.

The village people act as their own priests. A salaried priest, living in Udaipur, was invited on special occasions. Usually the villagers observed their religious practice in their own way. The Bible and the glories of god were published in Odia. Each one of them held a copy in their hands. Odissi *khola* and *madaka* musical instruments also infused some gaiety into the rituals. That day, a sixteen-year-old boy had been selected to read out the text. I liked that independent yet simple religious institute. The Christian ashram of Kodaikanal came to my mind. In the name of religion, all kinds of people from distant places congregated there. Perhaps the rich people came there for a change of place for a month. Most of them were rich. Only in the church they met each other with greetings from their inner being. The religious fervour in Chheligada was much greater than that of Kodaikanal. People who met each other every day and shared their daily life came to the church with absolute faith in God. The great soul was probably present in Chheligada, not in Kodaikanal.

It is likely that hints about future prosperity had been given to the poor, untouchable *paanas,* known as "paddy Christians", to convert them into the Royal Religion. Not just here in Ganjam, this practice has reigned from Australia to Africa. Many young Christians, depicting themselves as missionaries, have left their homes to establish an 'Empire of the Gospel.' These missionaries have left their footmarks even in China.

The world has left behind the passionate missionaries of the nineteenth century. Gone are those days when people were not enticed by the facade; human beings have crossed that limiting line and are now no longer weighing things on the scale of values. The emergent people of this century would do the same thing with the Buddha, Prophet Mohammed, Jesus Christ, and Sri Krishna. Earlier, whosoever worshipped whatever form in whichever place, cutting across barriers of belief, would have revered those who touched the innermost corners of the common man.

Though that past is gone, this Christian settlement was comparatively clean. The behaviour of the people was also polished. There was fellow-feeling and a communitarian spirit. One of the main characteristics of Christianity is following this spirit. This is one reason those missionaries have to be thanked. Due to their relentless and selfless service, today there is spread of education in our country; today, also they are making men healthy. Their patience and sincerity keep the wick of Christ lit.

The mass prayer was going on when suddenly some women shouted. I noticed a snake right over my head, suspended from the ceiling. Everyone stood up shouting. The black snake was killed with a wooden stick. Once again, prayers resumed.

We were invited to eat after our return from the church. Food was served in typical Odia style. I was pleased to eat the chicken and rice. I did not dare to hurt their sentiments by declaring that I was a vegetarian. The coward in me was defeated—it was the heart that won.

It was time to leave Chheligada, severing my new emotional ties. The villagers sent a boy to accompany me. I was once again on the road. There were still twelve kilometres to cover.

Up above, in the blue sky, played a few white clouds. The rain clouds were gathering again, above the deep valleys abutting the distant mountains. It was past noon. The total journey, of forty-eight kilometres, was going to end that day.

Suddenly, looking back, I saw two children running towards us. Of the two, I had known Kalinjan during the short stay. They carried instructions for my guide. "Never accept money if Babu gives it." I was really astounded at the affection and care of the poor people.

Kalinjan was then a young boy. He was hardly fifteen years old, but he was already married. Marriage was a simple event. Getting children married was just viewed as a duty to be performed by the parents. The boy accompanying me said he had been married for five years. At the age of eighteen, he was the father of a child.

His name was Gorakha. Talking of his sorrows and happiness, he bared his heart. During our conversation he revealed, "I was not initially willing to accompany you. I thought that you have come from Brahmapur and that you will speak English or Telugu. I thought that I will follow you from a distance, never coming close. Say whatever, our Odia is so clear no other language can match it."

I considered myself lucky for this union of our hearts.

Translated by **Rabindra Kumar Swain**
Excerpt from Ganjam Mala re Sata Dina
(Seven Days in Ganjam Highlands)

DIALOGUE: A Modern Philosophy of Life

Martin Buber, a professor of philosophy at the University of Jerusalem, passed away on the 13th of June 1965 at the age of 87. There are many reasons why I wish to introduce this philosopher from the distant mid-west to the readers of "Nabapatra". I believe that writers can effectively convey their experiences when they imagine themselves engaged in a conversation with their readers. Those who, driven by a desire for recognition and reputation, seek to dazzle and overwhelm the reader instead of engaging in a genuine conversation, may succeed in attaining a lofty position, much like Angad who created a seat for himself by growing and coiling his tail. However, such a writer will never truly engage in a meaningful exchange with another human being. One who propagates an ideology disguised as literature might gain fame for their talent but will not be acknowledged as wise or knowledgeable, as they fail to participate in genuine dialogue. It is through dialogue and discourse that literature takes shape, doors to knowledge open, societal change begins to unfold, and it becomes possible to transform the interconnected art of discovering life and the self into the art of expressing life itself.

In the *Bhagavat* and several other Puranas, we encounter instances of dialogue. We are all somewhat familiar with Krishna-Uddhav discourse or Narad-Parikshit discourse. However, in these 'dialogues', only one person engages in conversation; one poses inquiries while the other provides answers. Uddhav, the devout follower, consistently poses questions, and Sri Krishna, the ultimate source of all answers, responds to dispel any doubts in his devotee's mind. This cannot truly be classified as a dialogue. Rather, it could be considered sermon delivery and attentive listening. It resembles a speech rather than an exchange of thoughts. The presentation of these sermons evokes the feeling of being inside an Indian classroom, where the teacher speaks, and the students listen attentively. When one person speaks, the rest strive to maintain silence. In the *Bhagavat,* Uddhav and Parikshit are at least observed to be asking questions. However, in line with the standards of public conduct articulated in *Kali Bhagavat,* the natural and traditional practice of asking questions has been forsaken in our educational institutions.

In this essay, I shall utilise the terms "samvad" and "sambhashan" to convey the meaning of the English word "dialogue." The concept of 'dialogue' held significance in the theatre of ancient Greece. Within a theatrical production, dialogue is commonly perceived as an exchange between two individuals. This philosophy, advocated by Martin Buber, is recognized as the Philosophy of Dialogue. Buber regards the philosophy of dialogue as the foundation of a fruitful life. Scholars of philosophy worldwide may not formally acknowledge Buber's ideas as true philosophy. Literature can fail to captivate linguistics and grammar scholars, who employ rules to comprehend language and humanity. Similarly, philosophy instructors, specializing in the principles of philosophy, may find Buber's thoughts disagreeable. Hence, it should not be a cause for sorrow or surprise if Buber's name is absent from the philosophy departments of our universities.

Martin Buber was born into a Jewish family in Central Europe. During the latter half of the 19th century, the European continent was immersed in fervent nationalism. Deceptive nationalism typically manifests in two forms. Firstly, it involves an affectionate admiration for one's own race, regarding every accomplishment as significant and exceptional. Secondly, it encompasses a disdainful attitude towards individuals of other races, discrediting their achievements as inferior and meaningless. This disdain may serve as a compensatory support for the irrationality of jingoistic pride. Each advanced European race had its own nation: the Germans had Germany, the Italians had Italy, and the French had France. On the other hand, races such as the Polish and the Czechs struggled to liberate their countries from the dominion of larger nations. However, the Jewish people lacked a nation they could call their own, as they resided in numerous European countries without being recognised as citizens in any of them. They were devoid of the freedom to consider their place of birth as their homeland. Over the course of centuries, Jews faced scorn from Christians who accused them of deicide and subjected them to various forms of persecution. Consequently, amidst the surge of militant nationalism in Europe, animosity and hatred towards Jews escalated, leading to direct exploitation and physical assault. Such widespread scorn reduced them to a state of isolation from European society. Nevertheless, a small group of optimistic Jewish revolutionaries and intellectual leaders dreamt of returning to their homeland, Israel, to establish a new society.

It was within such a social milieu that Martin Buber was raised and educated. Such a milieu may have felt confining to him. Within this confinement, a Jewish boy would develop solely within his Jewish identity, limiting his imagination to the Jewish way of life. In essence, despite being born with innate human aspirations, he would be unable to aspire to be recognised as a human being within the broader human society.

During his early years, Martin Buber was profoundly influenced by the Jewish revival and the teachings of the Hasidic movement. Throughout history, the Jewish people had endured numerous natural calamities and had been expelled from their sacred land, subjected to insults and persecution in various countries across the globe. From the outset, Buber staunchly supported the Jewish yearning to return to their homeland and build a society based on their national religion and culture. In the eighteenth century, the Hasidic movement gained traction within Jewish communities in southeast Poland. This religious movement advocated for transcending dry and rigid rituals, emphasising instead a devout existence inspired by religious ideals. Buber translated several religious scriptures of the Hasidic faith, offered modern interpretations, and infused them with fresh inspiration and distinct characteristics. Buber did not view religion as a means of escaping worldly life or seeking refuge from the complexities of human existence through prayer and meditation. He believed that God is omnipresent and exists within this world. Consequently, to renounce the world would be to forsake the realm of God. True religion, according to Buber, entailed residing in the world and collaborating with fellow human beings to create a harmonious existence. In doing so, one would engage in various activities and fulfil their responsibilities as acts of devotion towards God. Every moment would hold eternal inspiration, every meaningful encounter would be imbued with divine inspiration, and every action would be guided by the call of religiosity. Buber believed that establishing truth and justice in this world was also a religious endeavour. God and His kingdom were not separate from the earthly realm, therefore the notion of entering heaven or the kingdom of God after death was merely an illusion. By fulfilling one's responsibilities, one could transform the essence of religion into tangible reality. Buber considered the purification of the world, society, and one's own life as the true manifestation of religion.

Martin Buber's philosophy is known as the "Philosophy of the Dialogue." He authored a book titled "I and Thou," in which he elucidates the relationship between humanity and the world as akin to the relationship between the self and another person. Buber asserts that no individual exists in isolation; likewise, no race or nation is detached from others, and no religion is fundamentally distinct from another. Man is intricately connected with the world he inhabits. When we encounter another human being, we address them as "thou." True dialogue can only occur between present individuals. To grasp the profound meaning of life and enrich our own existence, we must establish a relationship of "thou" with our surroundings and embrace the companionship of others. Buber posits that the relationship between God and man is predominantly one of "dialogue" as well. If we can perceive the divine essence permeating our environment, we can forge a bond of "I and Thou," recognising the shared humanity with others. We would treat different races and nations with the same respect we have for our own, and we would demonstrate reverence for other religions just as we do for our own. Regrettably, Buber laments the breakdown of "dialogue" or the "I-Thou" relationship in the modern world. People, races, and religions feel disconnected from one another. Individuals strive to outdo one another for selfish gains, while races seek to assimilate the essence of others. Buber labels this strained relationship as "I-It" or "I-This." The most deplorable manifestation of this relationship arises when one human being views another as mere dust and stone, when one race subjugates another, or when one religion deems another as worthless and insignificant. In Buber's own words, "If an individual only maintains a self-centred relationship and constantly seeks to control, exploit, and use others as tools for personal service, their life can never be considered truly abundant."

While examining our own nation and society through the lens of this philosopher's perspective, it becomes apparent that a healthy and genuine "dialogue" has not yet taken root among the people of our nation. Any sporadic instances that do occur can be seen as exceptions rather than a prevailing tradition. If an "I and Thou" relationship was to be established among the people of our nation, one can imagine the transformative impact it would have on our lives. In our country, politics often views people not as individual human beings, but as a faceless mass. The laws of the land do not treat each person as inherently valuable. The leaders of our nation have never felt compelled to engage in dialogue with the citizens. Similarly, within offices, if senior officials and supervisors were to initiate a "dialogue" with junior staff, clerks, and attendants, one can envision the positive changes that would unfold within the office environment. If educators embraced "dialogue" as the guiding principle of education, they would start perceiving students as individuals with boundless potential. Our focus would shift away from the mere passing or failing of students and instead emphasise cooperation for the development of human lives. By engaging in a lively "dialogue" with life and the natural world around us, our literature would also become more potent. Instead of seeking validation from the ruling elite or vying for a place in ostentatious gatherings, our literature would derive strength and pleasure from pleading for a genuine connection with life itself.

The relationship of "I and Thou" is inherently one of love and affection. When we engage in such a relationship, it is our responsibility to treat the other person with care and consideration. If we view someone as a slave or as a mere object, devoid of value, how can genuine affection exist? The most expansive form of this love is to extend it to every human being and hold accountable our own self for the well-being of everyone. Unfortunately, as materialism has gained prominence in our world, human beings have also become objectified. Love itself has been commodified. We treat knowledge as a commodity, engaging in its buying and selling. In our quest to analyse objects, the human mind has also objectified religion and God. In our pursuit of power and control, we have even devised plans for the destruction of human beings. We are now plotting to annihilate hundreds of thousands of people. The supposedly knowledgeable individuals sit in scientific laboratories, detached from the consequences, developing weapons of mass destruction. Such actions would not have occurred if there had been a sense of 'I-Thou' relationship among humans, fostering genuine connection and empathy.

Just as it is in the wider world, the same dynamics

can be observed within our own homes. If the master and mistress of the house establish an "I-Thou" relationship with the young servant who diligently carries out household tasks, recognising his humanity above all else, they would feel a sense of responsibility towards him. The fact that the boy is deprived of attending school and is compelled to perform menial chores is a flaw in our social system, and the master and mistress would acknowledge their own accountability for this situation.

Similarly, if a fortunate young man attending college feels compelled, by the fortunate circumstances of his own life, to establish an "I-Thou" relationship with a dark-skinned boy who shines his shoes, he would be able to witness the profound suffering ingrained in the core of the latter's being. As a result, he would start viewing himself as responsible for addressing this plight. Revolution is not simply a matter of heads rolling. Throughout history, oppressive leaders have resorted to beheading individuals to quell revolutions. Driven by their thirst for power, they have considered people as worthless and have led them from one period of darkness to another. The perspective of "I-Thou" or a compassionate outlook may perhaps offer a more reliable path towards revolution, one that acknowledges the inherent worth and interconnectedness of all individuals.

Twelve years ago, I had the opportunity to spend a few months in Italy. Additionally, I visited Jerusalem with the hope of meeting Martin Buber at a place of great significance to three religions. Filled with apprehension, I composed a letter, asking if such a learned man would spare some time for an Indian student. Promptly, I received a reply stating, "Come in the evening on such and such day, as I have no other commitments then." On a wintry night, resembling a pilgrim, I arrived at Martin Buber's doorstep. Despite his age of seventy-five, Buber exuded the spirit of a young scholar-philosopher. Welcoming me into his home, Buber engaged in conversation until midnight. Martin Buber did most of the talking, while I assumed the role of a humble listener. The room was adorned with countless books, its walls seemingly submerged in literary works. Amidst the literary sea, there existed a small table occupying a slightly empty space. For years, it had served as Martin Buber's arena for engaging in a "dialogue" with the world through his thoughts. In matters concerning religion, philosophy, social consciousness, and education, he maintained a friendly connection with the global human family through dialogue.

As I listened, all my trivial concerns melted away. It felt as though my self-deprecating thoughts and memories had dissipated into the ether. Despite the considerable age gap of over half a century between Martin Buber and myself, on that day when I sat before him, it was as if I had been reborn, embracing a new identity that transcended nationality and sect.

On that day, I envisioned Erasmus (Desiderius Erasmus Rotterdamus) in Martin Buber. Allow me to remind you of the erudite visionary who, in the face of Martin Luther's ascent and his movement to intertwine religion with greed for power and animosity towards humanity, advocated for a humanistic approach to the religious renaissance. Martin Buber had been deeply interested in studying various events in India. He retrieved two essays from one of his old books and presented them to me. One essay was written during a disagreement between Mahatma Gandhi and 'Deshabandhu' Chittaranjan regarding the path to be pursued for the freedom movement. The second essay was composed during the Second World War. We are all aware of how Hitler spearheaded a movement in Germany to exterminate Jews. During that time, Gandhi urged the Jews to embrace civil disobedience (*satyagraha*) and non-violent resistance (*ahimsa*) as a response to the brutal autocratic rule. In contrast, Buber argued that such methods would prove ineffective against the calculated and merciless murder of the Jews. Buber contended that for satyagraha and ahimsa to succeed, the opposing party must possess a modicum of compassion, no matter how small. Generally, the Jews had obediently followed Hitler's orders without protest or rebellion. Whether non-violent resistance and disobedience against Hitler's murderous regime could have justified their sacrifices remains a subject of debate.

The endeavour to lead a life based on justice is deemed a religious approach, as per Martin Buber. It falls within the remit of religion to empower and inspire such an endeavour. A truly religious individual will not shy away from disorder and will not selfishly confine themselves to the safety of prayer alone. To establish justice, they will actively engage with the world, fortified by renewed faith and sincerity. We observe such manifestations of religious devotion in the lives of Swami Vivekananda, Mahatma Gandhi, and Vinoba Bhave in India. Martin Buber ardently pursued peace for the world and was even bestowed a special award by Germany for his peace-making efforts. Nevertheless, for him, peace does not entail turning a blind eye to the injustices and inequalities prevalent in the world. In his own words, "The world's objective is peace, and justice is the path to peace." Justice, in this context, does not signify the oppression of majority opinions.

According to Buber, justice entails promoting equality among individuals and fostering a social environment that facilitates "dialogue" among human beings.

Martin Buber, being Jewish, faced numerous attempts by contemporary Europe to confine his identity solely to being a Jew. In response, Buber demonstrated his identity as a global citizen, showcasing his capabilities not only as a prominent Jew but also as an exceptional human being. Today, his thoughts and perspectives assume great significance and relevance for all of us. Those individuals who perceive life as a vocation and consider establishing connections with fellow human beings as the greatest calling of all would find immense inspiration in Buber's philosophy of "dialogue." In our society, poets, writers, educators, and politicians who intend to acknowledge and embrace individuals as they are, and who view the pursuit of wholehearted engagement with all as the ultimate goal of youth, should initiate a "dialogue" within their respective communities. They should transcend the narrow mindset of "I-It" and establish relationships based on an "I-Thou" connection. If Martin Buber were alive in our country, he would offer such advice.

Translated by **Urmishree Bedamatta**
As essay from 'Kete Diganta' (Many Horizons)

Forty Years Later

In August 1945, on the instructions of the US government, two atomic bombs were dropped on two cities in Japan. Such a terrible weapon had not been used in any previous warfare. The first bomb was dropped on the Japanese city of Hiroshima and the second on another city, Nagasaki. On August 6th and 9th respectively, these two bombs were dropped on the residents of the two cities from an aircraft. It was not as though such an innovative new weapon was used to defeat Japan in the war. By that time, the Japanese government had accepted defeat and offered to surrender. However, military scientists persuaded the government to use the bomb. The bombs were dropped so that the scientists making the bombs would get to observe the actual results from the application of this new technology. The scientists hoped that this evidence would help develop even more powerful nuclear bombs in the future. Why would the government not have agreed to this?

What was the consequence of dropping the two atomic bombs? The number of casualties was calculated and released for the public. In this attack, one hundred twenty thousand people died in Hiroshima. Seventy-eight thousand people lost their lives in Nagasaki. But what happened to the person who was sent to Japan to drop the bomb?

One of the flight attendants on that infamous campaign was Claude Eatherly. A team dropped two new bombs on the two target cities. Arrangements had been made to honour them as "national heroes" upon their return to the United States. But ultimately, what was the suffering Eatherly would undergo?

On returning to America, Eatherly realized he was no longer the same person. He had undergone significant changes. Perhaps, he experienced that he encountered his own ghost when he looked at himself. His outward appearance also changed in such a way that even his closest friends could not easily recognize him. He began sitting silently, as though he meant to discourage any conversation. He reduced all social interaction with his friends. A deep sense of hopelessness and helplessness enveloped him.

In 1947, Eatherly retired from his military career and moved to his place of birth located in the state of Texas. He was eligible for a pension, but he declined it. He contemplated returning all the medals and awards he had received from the government for his service in the war department, but his friends dissuaded him from doing so. As soon as the word Hiroshima was uttered, he would become very frightened. He would experience intense sadness and shame. If someone called him a hero during the war, he would lower his face in shame and leave the place. As soon as someone asked him about Hiroshima and Nagasaki, it was as though he could not answer at all.

Eatherly began sending money regularly to the mayor of Hiroshima. He used to send the money for the children who lost their parents in the nuclear bombings. He once wrote a letter to the members of the Hiroshima City Council confessing that he had played a major role in the bombing of Hiroshima and the events that followed; he had given the final signal to drop the bomb. In Eatherly's opinion, he was a criminal, responsible for the devastation and misery in Hiroshima.

After retirement, Eatherly wandered around looking for a job that would sustain him financially since he had declined his pension. He also tried to enrol in a university and pursue higher education. None of these ideas gave him the peace he sought. Finally, he resorted to drinking and gambling. He could not escape the haunting memories of his sordid act. His fear haunted him like a ghost to such an extent that he often cried out in his sleep. "The children are getting burnt, save them, save them", he would scream. In 1950, he attempted suicide.

Since dropping the bomb on Hiroshima was not recognized as a crime by his country, Eatherly did not receive any punishment. He yearned for it, thinking that some form of punishment would help him atone for his misdeeds.

He knowingly committed many crimes and courted arrest. His wish was fulfilled; he ended up in court. He was convicted and sentenced to prison. Later, he was declared mentally unwell, released from prison, and sent to an appropriate facility for treatment. A filmmaker promised Eatherly a hundred thousand dollars in exchange for his permission for a movie based on his life, but he did not accept the offer. His life ended in that facility.

Translated by **Ashim Kumar Sabat**
An Essay from Satyabrata's Dilemma

Notes from a Diary (School of Life)

16 January 1955

I had the good fortune of spending a day with Vinoba Bhave in Bankura, West Bengal. Gathering the savings of each day, Man goes on a pilgrimage. He washes the dust accumulated on him for so long in this place of pilgrimage. He comes back after purifying himself in this place. Encountering Mahatmas (great souls) is as good as seeing holy places on a pilgrimage. Man's life becomes purified through association with a Mahatma. By simply listening to the words spoken by a Mahatma, a lot of dirt and lies in one's speech get removed. Perhaps, great men take birth to remove the dirt in the minds of ordinary men, to break their illusions, and to prepare them for a life of beauty and *Dharma*.

Sankaracharya has spoken of the human body as a temple. But we cannot say that everybody's body is a temple. We pollute the place of devotion in us with so much blind attachment and broken faith. There the Divine does not feel enshrined; he perhaps leaves feeling humiliated. In His place, our attachment and pride occupy the throne. Only those who offer their life for God's work leaving behind their attachments and all forms of madness can be said to possess bodies as pure as temples. Likewise, upon seeing Mahatmas, devotion springs, eliminating the dirt and dust. One feels as though he may be standing in the vicinity of God's temple. Seeing Mahatmas makes Man discover and purify himself. The selfishness and ego that encase our true selves are cracked open. Meeting Vinoba was such an experience for me.

17 January 1955

It is often hard to make education age appropriate. Many complain that education is not able to prepare us for what our age needs.

It would be an injustice to term such a thing as education whose only objective is to make man appropriate for the needs of the age. A beast also adapts itself to what circumstances require of it. To calm its hunger and thirst, a beast eats food and drinks water. To save itself from the cold, heat, and rain, an animal takes shelter under a tree or in a cave. Therefore, the animal also adapts to Nature or its environment.

Man cannot be satisfied by eating, drinking, sleeping, and laughing alone. Human existence cannot be so limited. Man has given so much of joy, sadness, and compassion in all his works and with this has been able to thread them together as part of a special relationship. From these relations have arisen man's affection, love, and Dharma; human life has become delightful.

Man does not evolved by adapting to circumstances alone; he changes the circumstances according to his taste or choice and perspective. Destroying old conditions, he creates new ones. Ergo, his education ought to match this goal. Man's perspective, imagination, and thirst for work have been giving life ever-new colours and meaning.

Just becoming fit for contemporary times, one cannot think one's education complete and appropriate. We must receive epoch-changing education. Breaching the boundaries of our pond like existence, we must create new creative streams. In our lives, in every moment of in our daily lives, the old should be broken down, and newly created; the discarding of the old and the creation of new should continue. Then only is our education meaningful. Whether basic or advanced, national or foreign setting, all teachers and students need to keep this in mind. We would not be just useful to our times, like an animal; we will not be confined to the ignoble necessity of merely adapting to the environment. We will create an epoch.

18 January 1955

Our thoughts may be many, but our desire should be one; this is what Vinoba said in a worker's meet in Bankura. One is not immediately able to understand the meaning of this sentence. One must think deeply. Then only can we reach the essence of his statement. One can see that this has significance not only in the lives of the workers of Bhoodan Yagna, but in the lives of all men. It can also be applied in this little world of ours where every day each one of us is dreaming of a beautiful world and for this, we are moving forward.

With what desire have we come here? Come, let us ask this question in our hearts for a moment. The scene around here is very beautiful. But have we come here only to look at the beautiful scenery? After we move past the basic level of existence, our respect in society will be enhanced. The value of our education would increase. But have we come here to get the respect of five or more people and to earn more money? A life of study is a life of much fun and enjoyment. The government would help us month after month. But have we come here with greed to enjoy ourselves for four years with money pouring in from outside? Let us all ask this question within our families—teachers and students, elder and younger brothers.

No educational institution can run as a factory where wages are given in lieu of labour. It can never be a leisure garden of enjoyment. Then what is it? Those who come here, with what desire do they come here? But if you give me the right to tell you, then I will say: let us all do here the *sadhana* required to become a good person. We have come here with the aspiration to become a good person. Let us remind each other of this every day. We will stay here with a healthy body and healthy mind. We will all become *sarasa* (delightful); we will help others to become *sarasa* (delightful). We will wish well to those who are moving ahead. We will offer our hand and pick up the ones who are falling behind and make them equal. We all— yes, both teachers and students—are travellers in one path, friends of the path. Because the *sadhana* of becoming a good person did not end with any of us nor it would ever end. Neither for the student nor for the teacher. The desire that has brought us together, let this desire keep us affectionate and tolerant friends.

27 January 1955

Yesterday we had our Republic Day. Possibly many of us wished to celebrate the day properly and wanted to celebrate a festival of joy and arrange meetings and so on. But we did not celebrate our Republic Day by raising flags or singing the national anthem. We are all studying now. We are all children. There are also those who are younger than us. So far under the sky in our country, there have been no houses made for them. For many of them, it is still too much to ask whether they have food and clothes. Would children in such a country study where they are polishing shoes to satisfy their hunger, begging naked on the street corner, and carrying our burdens as coolies? We must do *sadhana* for many more years for all the children of our country to rightfully come to schools.

If the democracy of the country was real, then the real men of the country would have experienced this. It would not have been necessary to observe the Republic Day by putting out a government notification. Such practices do not happen either in Denmark or in the USA. There, everybody labours equally, studies freely, and speaks their mind as equals. There, human beings are accorded the dignity of human beings; they are given proper education. Everybody loves children thinking of them as the commons of the entire country... we have a long path to traverse to bring about such conditions in our country.

Before we received our political independence, we were also celebrating January 26 as our national festival. People of India used to take a vow to free our country. All were taking a resolution that we have the right to live as human beings, we are ready to surrender everything to make us free. We have been pledging that after independence, we would build a new society and system based upon truth and non-violence. We have now come far away from the path of *ahimsa* or non-violence. Now, the resolution about *ahimsa* or non-violence has been removed from our letter of vow. Before celebrating January 26, every student must think deeply about it.

Translated by **Ananta Kumar Giri**

Excerpts from Jeevana Vidyalaya (School of Life)

A window into the world: Two Essays

I

I am in my home. The continuous flow of life surrounding me is the world as portrayed in books. I am happy within my own little space and forget that others who are outside are really there. Most of us who believe in God are convinced that we have been sent to earth to live our own lives. I must therefore live my life according to my own reasoning. As much as possible, I should insulate and secure my home. I will consider it my achievement and be pleased with it. Those who worship God so passionately refer to him as the Creator, the Saviour, or the Lord of the Universe in a habitual manner. They are nevertheless preoccupied with their own issues, and their prayers are limited to their own troubles. They completely forget that life provides a window to view the world. Perhaps they wonder whether their little heads have sufficient space to contemplate both their own lives and the rest of the world at once. Certainly, they are not capable of achieving such a feat.

There are many people who believe they are living a happy life within their own little enclosures. In their view, they possess just the amount of power necessary to create and maintain their little worlds. In their minds, they see themselves as a cow or a calf tethered to a pole by some mysterious force. Since both the pole and the rope are short, their circumference must be small. They do not wish to contemplate why God has restricted them in this manner, as though they are living moment-by-moment. Why would the happy calf— tied to a small pole with a short rope—bother to realize that each moment is preceded by many such moments and that we are engulfed by a great moment which binds them all together? The world of happy people nurtures a particular prejudice— the greater your intellect, the sadder your life will be. The wise among us have warned that as the circle of life increases, life will become increasingly challenging for us. Because of this, the pole and rope are short, and the circumference is thereby limited. From within, our little conscience assures us that comfort lies within this restricted space. Attempting to widen one's eyes— to look farther or deeper— will only increase one's worries; nothing else will be accomplished. There is no way one can change this world.

Upon reaching this point, all arguments are rendered ineffective. This world cannot be changed by humans. Humans are small when compared to the vastness of the universe. The little human believes that his fate is greater than him, and his world is even greater than that. It is fate that prompts him to dance, triggers a fall, and enables him to rise again. He keeps rolling from one place to another due to fate alone. He can never determine his fate, and it is even more difficult to alter it. Planets and stars shape a person's fate. A bleak future awaits when Saturn gets furious, while Jupiter's blessings can turn a dead tree green. These insights come from astrology. Not only in India, but in most countries around the world, this science has existed throughout history. It exists in our time. Throughout history, that same sheep has changed its coat and sagely urged humans to accept their fate and confinement. The sages of our time refer to this as existentialism. Neither you know where you have come from nor where you are going. Your head is weighed down by a large rock. Why have you been burdened with this rock is beyond your comprehension. You are at the base of a mountain. With this rock on your head, you must reach the summit. You anticipate reaching the summit soon and placing the rock down to end all of your miseries. Before that happens, you will drop the rock and watch it roll back towards the mountain base. Once again, you must lift, climb, and ascend. In essence, this is what makes up your life. It is impossible to do otherwise. You will end up losing if you chart a different course for yourself. No one has investigated who forces you to climb and ascend a mountain while weighed down by a huge rock. No one knows which crown awaits should you pass this test. It is possible that no one is forcing you to do so. The process is automatic. This is the Truth. Accept this Truth and be happy with it. Seek no further than this. In the event that you try, you are likely to be disappointed and end up nowhere.

Due to these ominous words, one decides to be content within one's small space. Still, when I look inside, it appears as though a window has opened. Through that window, I can see the entire universe. There is no longer a rock nor a mountain. I no longer humiliate myself by performing the same exerting task over and over again. In a sense, I feel entangled in all of this via a thousand strings. I do not know which of my friends arrives at the right time to open the window.

(04/08/87)

II

Where can one find a window? The window has no location. When one seeks, one can find a window. One discovers the sky only after seeking it out. The truth lies nowhere. As soon as one begins to search for it, it begins to appear. We see it externally, feel it internally, and see it manifest in our relationships. While we read about the truth in the books, the truth does not exist in the books. Truth exists in life. It is only through living that truth can be experienced. In our world, many people are regarded as idealists. Idealists talk about ideals. They passionately argue that unless such and such ideals are in place, the world cannot emerge from its misery. For at least an hour, they inspire us with their speech. A person may be an idealist, but it does not mean they are intimately acquainted with the ideals they espouse. The situation is analogous to the situation of someone who worships God but does not experience proximity to him. In order to perceive an ideal, one must live it.

Whenever we open a window in our lives, we begin to see more than we are used to within the confines of our daily lives. In general, what we perceive and experience about ourselves is limited in scope. As we look up around us, does the sky seem as vast as it really is? Five hundred years ago, humans believed that the earth was as large as they perceived it to be. The earth appeared to them to be flat, and they held this belief to be true. According to them, those who believed the earth was round were insane. People with differing opinions were punished. Throughout history, elders in our society have viewed us as being small and insignificant. How can a few elders claim respectability if the small and minor ones are not in greater numbers? In case teachers in our schools stop referring to children as insignificant and lesser, will children still regard them as gurus? Unless minors are socialized to view themselves as minors, how can elders assert their authority over them? It has been this way for centuries in our world. Based on this perspective, it should be obvious why it was necessary to keep most people's windows closed. There is no doubt that only when the windows of the vast majority of the population are closed, the burrows of society's elite who are in minority will appear deeper.

Is it really true that people keep their windows closed? No, they also move about this world. They build relationships and attempt to bring far-off things closer. To fetch water, they connect pipes. However, they remain confined to their own burrows. Every morning, they emerge from their burrows and return to them at night. They keep their burrows covered because they believe it is essential for their safety. As if they had learned this from *Vyasa Deva* himself, they emphasize and adhere to this practice with the greatest attention. Such persons can be found everywhere, as if they are frantically seeking to take up every available space. Their real windows are closed. To be more precise, they never want to open their windows. Though they appear to move about among everyone in society, they are not actually present anywhere. They stay hidden inside their burrows. They are present in the realms of religion, ethics, and education. They are also present in the opposite axis, which has sin, immorality and propaganda. They are like horses on the run. Even so, they remain inside their burrows, performing all sorts of calculations. As if they were married to the burrow, they are always engaged in its maintenance. When they open their so-called windows, they see only themselves instead of the sky.

When they agree to remove their dearly cherished covers from the burrows, the path towards opening the actual windows becomes clear. It is not uncommon for us to pretend to open our windows when an outsider asks us to do so. However, the real covers are only removed when we intend to remove them. Once they have been opened, they cannot be closed, even if the guru himself directs the closure. It is then that one becomes aware of the presence of the supreme guru within oneself. Defying all outer gurus, one wishes to adhere to the inner guru's words. The courage required for such adherence comes from within.

Real windows have two functions. When viewed closely, they constitute two sides of the same process. First, it brings the outside to the inside. The second function is to extend the inside to the outside. A mirror outside allows the inside to be viewed. The mirror inside also reflects the outside. The love of the outside entices the inside, and the love of the inside entices the outside. With the cover removed, it does not require a lot of effort. Both the outside and the inside are not afraid of each other. Others who exist in the world seem friendly. The problems of the world seem to be our personal challenges. So, we do not wish to ignore them. The challenges of life are perceived as a means of ascending the stairway of life. We feel happy about life. Both the outside and the inside feel good. *Tato na vijugupsate.*

(12/08/87)

Translated by **Biswajit Apat**
Essays from 'Biswa ku Gabakhya'
(A Window into the World)

Reflection on Shrimad Bhagabad Geeta

About five hundred years ago in Odisha, a great movement for the synthesis of prevalent religions, such as Vedic, Tantric, Buddhist, and Vaisnavism started. The Panchasakha, the collective of five saints in Odia Literature, was the mainspring of that movement. These five gems were Balaram, Jagannath, Jasobanta, Shishu Ananta, and Achyutananda. Their spiritual growth deeply influenced the religious life in Odisha.

Balaram was the oldest of the five poets. It is said that by the time Sri Chaitanya reached Puri *Shrikshetra* to propagate his religion, Balaram Das was already an adult. He accompanied Sri Chaitanya to the Deccan lands on a pilgrimage, as has been mentioned in the *Baisnaba Karacha*, a Vaishnavite treatise.

Balaram Das' date of birth cannot be ascertained with accuracy. So we have to base our date on the few facts from the concluding portions or chapters with the details of the poet and Abakash (hymns to deities) of their *pothis*. It is a fact that during the reign of Pratapa Rudra Deva, Balaram had displayed the talent of his *sadhana* (spiritual attainment) at Puri. In the 17th year of Pratapa Rudra's reign, that is in 1510, Balaram had read his *Gupta Geeta* at the *Mukti Mandap*. He must have been famous by that time. It is known from the *Dandi Ramayan* that he was around 33 by the time he completed the composition of the treatise.

It has been proved that Chaitanya had arrived in Odisha in 1509; by that time, Balaram's talent and sadhana was prolifically manifest. Though he was of Chaitanya's age, Balaram had initiated him. Among the Panchasakha, only Balaram's name is found in Bengali scriptures. From this, it is conjectured that Balaram Das was born between 1460-70 AD.

Most writers on the matter opine that Balararn Das was "*Karan*" by caste. But in all his *pothis* he has mentioned that he was a *sudra* (a low varna) (*Muhim papi hina. bisesh sudra*). Nagendranath Basu claimed that Balaram was an untouchable. In his *pothi- Ganesh Bibhuti,* Balaram has mentioned many things about the origin and place in society of the *Bauri caste* (an untouchable caste). In the "Abakash" of the Bhagbad Geeta, some hints are available about his belonging to the *Bauri caste* (*Jebe Brahmavidya kahuchhanti gopyakari / Kali Debarchana bele kahibi Bauri - Abakash*).

It is mentioned in many books by the Panchasakha that Somanath Mohapatra and Mahamaya or Manomaya were Balaram's parents. It has also been mentioned in the third chapter of his *Bhagabad Geeta* (*Mohapatra Somnath Tanaya Balaram adhyatma*). This Somanath Mohapatra was a minister of Kapilendra Dev, King of Odisha. Balaram Das's native village— Chandrapur in Puri district— is very close to Puri Srikshetra.

(*Namati Balarama Das/ Mahanta Somnath Shishya Purusottama Tava/ Kutumba Gheni nirantara*)

Therefore, Balaram must have visited Puri in his childhood and been drawn to the assembly of scholars. No information about his life before Chaitanya's time is available. Several scriptures only mention that he joined Sri Chaitanya after the latter's arrival at Puri. Sri Chaitanya initiated (*nama dikshya*) himself on his own. Iswar Das's Chaitanya Bhagabat is the only authentic book about Chaitanya's divine leela in Orissa (*Ramataraka Parambrahma/ Kahile Karne Srichatanya Sunina Balaram Das/ Manare hoile harasa*). Chaitanya whispered the name of Ram in his ear and Balaram Das heard it and became ecstatic.

We will later assess Balaram Das›s position as a religious preceptor. Let us now critically appreciate him as a poet and writer. There have been many discussions on the production of Sanskrit literature; such discussions had been traditionally monopolised by Brahmins. Non-Brahmins were prevented from listening to scriptures and puranas. But since 12th century AD, a greater enthusiasm could be sensed about vernacular languages. Religious preceptors started accepting this novelty while preaching religion. Perhaps Sarala Das's *Mahabharat* had taken pioneering steps in this direction, though there is proof of different 'koilis' and 'chautisas' in vogue. But the latter can't be accepted as folk songs.

Balaram Das is the precursor of this movement. Though his identity in history is more as a sadhak and passionate devotee, his identity as a poet is also widely recognised. His language is very simple, which resembles the language of the heart. His writing does not exhibit any flamboyancy or gaudiness in language to establish the quality of his composition. In those days, he emerged as a brilliant example of using vernacular to create meaningful literature.

It is uncertain till today as to how many *pothis* in all were written by Balaram Das. Certainly numerous such documents have remained under wraps by his devotees and priests than have been published. A list of *pothis* written by Odia poets as prepared by Hunter appears in Jagabandhu Singh's *Prachin Utkal*. In the text, it is seen that Balaram Das has written the following *pothis* : *Bedha Parikrama, Arjun Geeta, Bhaba Samudra, Bhagabad Geeta, Bhakti Rasamruta, Bhutakele, Virata Geeta,Chandipurana, Nama RatnaGeeta, Ramayan, Rasakeli, Sarira Bhagola, Chhatish Geeta, Gaja Nistaran Gita, Chhatish Geeta, Chandi Purana , Namaratna Geeta, Garuda Geeta, Bhakti Rasamruta. Bhutkeli.Gupta Geeta, Krishnaleela, Mahabharat, Mrugunistuti, Rasa Binod, Tulabhina, Geeta Saar.* In fact, the list also contains the names of some *pothis*, not composed by Balaram Das. For instance, *Rasa Binod* was written by Dinakrishna Das. The list prepared by Pandit Binayak Mishra mentions some more *pothis* such as *Brahma Purano, Kanta Koili, Laxmi Purana, Durga Stuti, Kamala Lochan Choutisa, Baramasi, Sabha Binod, Amar Kosha Geeta, Baula Gai Geeta*, etc. *Ramabibha* by Arjun Das has also been erroneously incorporated into that list.

Most importantly, Balaram's writings contain the examples of ancient Odia prose literature. In fact, Brajanath Badajena has been considered as the progenitor of ancient Odia prose literature. Though *Madala Panji* is written in prose, it is not literature. It cannot be taken for granted that the chronicle's language might not have been interpolated by later writers. The edicts of the 12th century AD that have come to light cannot also be included in literature. *Prachin Gadya— Padyadarsha* edited by Artaballav Mohanty and published by the Prachi Samiti— is a collection of illustrative ancient Odia literature. It has extracted a sample of prose piece from Brahma Geeta.

Narayan Abdhut Swami's *Rudra Sudhanidhi* contains some passages though its editor himself is sceptical about its date of composition and has claimed that the writing could have been produced in the 13th or 14th or 17th century. The *pothi* discussed as literature is the gem of that race and language. Hence, if *Rudra Sudhanidhi* or *Brahma Geeta* are published in their entirety, finding the genesis of Odia prose would become easier. So, Balaram Das's *pothi Ganesh Bibhuti*, should be considered as evidence of the most ancient Odia prose. Basu has discovered at Badasahi, Siddhanta *Dambaru*— an annotated *pothi* on Ganesh Bibhuti. Balaram Das himself has written this in both prose and poetry. Its summary has been written in prose at first, then it has been explicated in lucid poetry. Since both prose and poetry have been used at the same place, it may be accepted as belonging to the beginning of the age of prose. Balaram Das must have been bold enough to explicate religious doctrines in vernacular, making it equally excellent with verse. If a comprehensive history of that age is written, then it would come to light the kind of satire flung at him by Brahmin pundits. He has also discovered *Pranala Geeta* or *Pralamba Geeta*, the manuscript of another *pothi* by Balaram Das at the Mukti Mandap. Prachin Utkal has also mentioned that Balaram Das composed another *pothi* in prose titled *Gyana Chudamani*.

Most people, who have used vernacular instead of Sanskrit as the medium of expression of literature, barring a microscopic minority, are non-Brahmins. The surname of Sarala Das's lineage is Parida . Balaram himself has said that he was a '*Shudra*'. Jasobanta and Achyutananda were born in Kshyatriya and Gopal (milkman) families respectively. History has indicated that Brahmins had monopolised the study of Sanskrit and confined the knowledge to their section. The King at that time was also afraid of them. No branch of knowledge was open to common men. Religion and practice of religion were only Brahmin's theory and the Mukti Mandap's hereditary property.

At that time, the Kings of Orissa indulged in war campaigns. In fact, that was the darkest age for the uneducated and uncultured common men. Accompanying all discontent and backwardness, a group of life-oriented poets, despite becoming eyesores for the king, opened the hidden chamber of knowledge, wrote content about indigenous thought and in common man's language. Thus began a new flood. Scriptures were written based on the language and profession of the society. The metaphysics of religion was propagated using spoken language in vogue. Literary gymnastics at the expense of thought was not undertaken anymore. Perhaps the history of all languages has passed through such transitions. Breaking the slumber of the classic age and penetrating the roots deep into the soil, vernacular has expressed itself spontaneously. From this point of view, the phase from the Age of Sarala to the Age of Panchasakha is extremely significant in Odia literature.

Some examples of the use of prose (in vernacular) *Ganesh Bibhuti* and *Siddhanta Dambaru* are cited: *"Om Namah Omati . Ehanu japisthira Karib. Paban toliba . Surya ghare rahiba. E mantra japa kale dhuni Madhye shabad shubhiba. Kabi Pandit sarbagya tinipada paaiba. Om Ram om Ram . Ehaku pabana tolilabele japa kale paban sthira huai. E je ulat hoiachhi. Chandrayanare Ramanama japiba/ Suryayana hele Mara boli japiba. Padmalayaputra Dola bauri atanti /Brahmana sange Veda padhuthanti / Brahman jyestha/ Bauri Kanistha. E Veda padhuthile/ Prataprudrankatharu gupta kari Brahmane rakhichhanti/ Kaliyuge na chhuile, Bauriku chhuinle sakal patak kshaya heba / Ethi jogu Visnu mayakari rakhiachhanti/ Suna ho Ganesh Bada gahan eha gupta kari thoibu/ sethi jogu Brahman Bauri gaar livai na paranti/ Murdhapata hebe boli shapya maniachhanti/ Padmalaya putra Bayokandi Paramananda Bhoi Radhu Samal."*

Balaram Das's Ramayana and Geeta are very famous. Much discussion has been and will be done about them. But small *pothis* like *Kanta Koili Baula Gai,* etc. and hundreds of Bhajans (hymns) recited fondly by the public possess no less literary value. In every literature, it is found that people expressed their thoughts and emotions in folk songs, badinage, idioms, banters, dance, and songs before sambandha literature was written. Further, in every literature, certainly for composing numerous badinages and folk songs, no grammar or knowledge of rhetoric and prosody was thought mandatory. Since these literary forms made emotions as the basis of their rhythm and rhyme, they have been sung orally. Their genesis cannot be traced to any theory, but from the soul of a race. National poet Balaram had derived his language, rhythm, and soul from these folk songs. In fact, his hymns, devotional songs, chautisa and koilis are folk literature. This is why *Koilis, Baramasis,* and *Chautisas* have remained very dear to the soul of Odisha even after ages. Critical discussion of this literature will reveal the soul of the Odia nation.

Kanta Koili, Mruguni Stuti, Gaja Nistarana, Bhaba Samudra are based on "Karuna rasa" (pathos). The speciality of the Odia soul is to offer its devotion to its desired deity through the emotion of pathos (karuna rasa). The purest self of the Odia language gets its efflorescence when pathos (karuna rasa) is described. The pathos of the distressed has been liberally used in every *pothi* mentioned above. The pure flower of heart blossoms very easily only through the "Karuna rasa". And such surrender leads to the proper union of the self with the most desired. The description of Sita's wailing in *Kanta Koili,* the deer and the elephant's surrender in *Mruguni Stuti* and *Gaja Nistarana* are excellent, and they touch the innermost recesses of the Odia soul. *Baulagai Gita* (The Song of the Cow named Baula) may be taken to be a legend. It's an imaginary tale that narrates effectively on its every page the significance of Dana (sacrifice).

Balaram Das tried to locate all the places of pilgrimage in Orissa. It is possible for a national poet to exhibit his predilection for representing his motherland as the repository of all wonders. But he has not run to the Himalayas to locate Lord Shiva's sacred seat. He has attributed the divine-souled Himalayas to Kapilas in symbolism in Odia literature. The Absolute (Para Brahma) of Vedanta and Maha Sunya (great void) of Aadi Buddha of Buddhism have been fused into the image of Jagannath. Balaram, the devout (spiritual practitioner) sadhak was able to synthesise all religions and metaphysics of religions in this institution of Jagannath.

Translated by **Braja Mohan Mishra**
Excerpt from introduction to
Bhagavad Geeta by Balaram Das

Seeking Universalism: Festivals and Languages

I

Christmas can no longer be called the festival of western society or Christians alone. Festivals were not created to show that humans are different from one another. The Hindus of India celebrate Dussehra, while Muslims in the Middle East observe Muharram. Christians rejoice during Christmas. The purpose of a festival everywhere is to experience pleasure by indulging in different activities, and by establishing easy contact with other humans, to experience soul-satisfaction in this world beset with cares and anxieties.

It is our misfortune that we do not get enough inspiration from our festivals as we have forgotten their *raison d'etre.* By putting some festive days in our almanac or calendars, we feel proud that these are our festive days; others put some other days in their almanac and feel proud that those are their festival days. This false glorification separates men from one another. Man has segregated himself from others by assigning categories such as "Hindu", "Muslim", and "Christian". By erecting barriers through names such as Eastern, Western, old, and new, man has separated one culture from another.

These divisions explain why a Hindu fanatic takes certain pride in leading a Dussehra procession around a mosque, making sure his presence is registered through the relentless beating of drums. Another man wilfully sets up a butcher's trade in a manner that the daily slaughter of cows takes place right in front of a Hindu household. Man uses festivals like an intoxicant, to experience a certain release and a triumphant feeling. This type of self-satisfaction is self-degenerating. Consequently, religion and related festivals ultimately bring us sorrows and hatred instead of pleasure and amity. Our challenge today, as new men of a new world, is to reduce these divisions.

According to the Upanishads, the world of tomorrow will be "one single place" for man to live. The new man will no longer preserve regional or local artefacts and customs as his culture. As human beings of tomorrow, therefore, we will learn to accept all rituals and pleasure provided by all religions and cultures as our own. If we see from such a perspective, this joyous Christmas festival will also be our own.

None can decisively prove if Jesus was born on Christmas day in the village Bethlehem of Israel. A major festival was observed at the same time even in Pagan or unchristian societies much before Christianity arrived in Europe. It is possible that a pagan festival was instrumentalised to produce a sacred day to remember the birth of Jesus. In the cosmopolitanism era, the birth of Jesus won't remain a sacred day for only one community. All the people of this world will observe this festival. The birth of Jesus and his messages have not only benefitted one community but have inspired the whole of mankind. Today, it cannot be said that the Gita, the Bible, or the Tao Te Ching is the spiritual property of one religion or community. In this Age of Science, whatever can be universal will be called spiritual. A day might come when we can be intimate with those whom we have kept away by calling them Christians.

If the substance of Christianity is to love one's neighbour just like one's own, then I shall say there will be the dawn of good fortune for humans only when the entire world becomes Christian. Today, we only find fault with others. We see more and more the differences among us. We cannot feel that in all of us, there is a heart of truth and a pathetic history of stumbling and treading on the way. We are unable to feel it. Love man despite his myriad mistakes and weaknesses, just as the Buddha, Jesus, and Gandhi did.

On the one side we have the rules of judgement by the moralist, on the other side there are religious precepts to love more and make others as our own to a greater degree. Is not the history of the world chiefly the history of struggle between these two sides? Once Jesus had appeared to become the commander of the side of love in this struggle. In our times, Mahatma Gandhi had reawakened the case of Christ in Indian life. We are out to search for more and more love despite the jealousy. Therefore, we will observe the festival of the birth of Christ with the heart of a Christian. We will experience the story of Jesus's life in our hearts with the inspiration of a true Christian.

With the passage of time, Christmas festival has gradually become a familial ceremony. Folk culture has been united with religious culture to make Christmas more beautiful and enjoyable. To be more specific, it has become a festival of children. The entire month of December, too, gives immense pleasure to every Christian child. That is why the month of cold and snow becomes warm with the abundant joy of children. It becomes lively and noisy with universal joy.

This world is gradually becoming a playground for adults. The adults have gradually begun to show their tyrannical prowess in all the fields of life in the name of scriptures, reforms, and society. The present control of modern civilization is directly proportional to the snatching away of the children's world from them. Nobody is willing today to give time to make children naturally happy by allowing some amount of leisure, leaving aside our worries. We do not recognise at all that human life has a time for play and a time for development. It is because the adult mind is preoccupied with such ideas as 'proper', 'improper', 'good', 'bad', 'heaven' and 'hell'. Long before the child matures through economic and mental pressures surrounding him, we entrap him with the complexities of life. In our society there is no time to be a child, no time to play, no time to do mischief. Gradually, we also drive children away from our festivals and ceremonies. So, it has become very urgent for our society to remember Christmas as a festival for children.

A favourable field should be created in this country to provide ample scope to behave like children.

II

There are several languages in our world. In noted universities, Linguistics is taught as a special subject of higher education. The scholars conduct research on the rules of construction, deconstruction, and on the cultural and social influence of the formation of a language. Generally, people take great pride in their own language.

In Odisha, we have our Odia language. We know that there was a movement in erstwhile East Pakistan, now Bangladesh, to make Bengali a recognised language. Now several people are still in jail for recognition of Pakhtoon language in the western border of Pakistan. There is a great controversy among Odisha, Bengal, and Bihar over the songs and couplets of Buddhist Charyapada, a collection of lyrical poems written by followers of Buddhist Sahaja cult found in Nepal and Tibet. To deepen the controversy, some scholars are busy writing books. A language will be treated as old and therefore more distinguished, if comparatively old books are found in that language. If an old palm leaf manuscript is found, we all lay claim to it. We are caught in a race to prove that our language is old. We ought to remember the Language Commission Report and the consequent bickering that followed it.

In several cases, religion, ideology, politics, scriptures, literature, and language can work like opium for the human mind. This is a pattern one can detect in the world's cultural history. None of us can look past the embedded glory of a language. All of us feel there is something great in language beyond its functional aspect as the primary vehicle of expression.

We have made a lot of noise to prop up our mother tongue, the spoken language of our common people. We must admit that these feelings of pride and hurt are consequences of a current called nationalism that had inundated the world by making the motherland or native land a potent symbol. Nationalism originated in Europe in the last century. Some thoughtful people, who wanted the welfare of humanity, produced this current with honest aims. But that current energised the unworthy among us.

A current is supposed to flow and carry away something by its force. But we made the flow of our mother tongue stagnant, like a pond. While worshipping our own language, we looked down on other languages. We considered them lowly or insignificant. As a result, different conflicts and quarrels were created between speakers of different languages. Although man possessed a liberal vehicle of expression called language, his mind became largely closed, separated, and isolated.

We generally think that language is lifeless and impersonal, but it is not so. Odia language does not entail only the books written by few scholars. It is a vehicle that carries the happiness, sorrows, desires, and aspirations of one and a half crore people. The history of Odia language is not a lifeless account of what part of Odia language came from where and how different words were formed. It does not merely mean the elements of grammar. The meaning of the history of our language is the history of human beings of this state. Odia language should bind together one crore and a half Odias in one thread. Similarly, there are several crores of people who inhabit the Bengal, who back Bengali. If we treat human beings as our own, their language will be our own. We do not get enough pleasure from language as we have not been taught how to know the people of a country through the language of that country. To know a people, we have to learn their language. Then language learning will no more be difficult. It can be a remedy to expand our hearts. The more languages we learn, we can accept more countries, societies and human beings as our own; our hearts can be broadened more. If we can accept this mantra of language-learning we will not get the scope to think about the petty and harmful aspects, such as one language is better or worse, or more difficult or easier than another language. If we want to become friends with more and more people, we must learn more languages. Everyone needs to make such a vow in this age.

Once I was staying in an agriculturist's family in a village in Denmark. The name of the eldest son of the family was Yakob. He was about eleven or twelve years of age. One day his mother asked Yacob, "Well, tell me, to which nationality Chitta belongs?" Without any doubt, as if he knew, Yakob replied, "Danish". Mother asked, "How did you know?" Yakob replied immediately, "Chitta is speaking Danish language. His nationality must be Danish". I was taken aback, witnessing this understanding of language from a child.

Now there is a special subject called Comparative Linguistics in the field of language research. The main thing about it is comparative study of different languages. This subject has been created for research-based discussion on the similarities and differences regarding the construction, deconstruction, and development of two languages and how they are influencing each other's culture.

We can say that this is a good sign of the desire of people in this age that a man should be nearer to another man. Australia is far from India; Africa is far away from England. Still, a student of India is carrying on research on the primitive languages of Australia; another department has been opened in London University to study the languages of Africa. Now people want to be nearer to one other, to bind people living in far-off places in their hearts.

Odia language is the language of Odisha, this language has also several dialects. In Cuttack, the dialect is Kataki, Sambalpuri in Sambalpur and Ganjami in Ganjam. Even then, why should we think that we are different from one another? We will learn different dialects of Odisha; we must know the special and local features of each dialect. We must love the entire Odia language along with its different dialects. If we cannot do that, the society and culture of Odisha will be divided. We would not feel that we are one.

Champatimunda, 1957

Translation by **Bijaya Kumar Nanda**
Two essays from 'Sila o Salagram'
(A stone and a Salagrama)

The Story of Ekalabya

In high schools in Uttar Pradesh, English literature textbooks include the story of Ekalabya. This story has been written by Annie Besant, who is a source of inspiration. Though brought up with Western values, Indian culture has opened before her vistas of human values, unique visions of enlightenment, and profundities of culture. And she has made a wholehearted endeavour to establish them as a unique way of life.

There is little doubt that every Indian child knows Ekalabya's story, appreciating its nuances before coming across it in school textbooks. Ekalabya hails from the Sabara tribe and is an outcaste. Yet he thirsts for learning. During his search for a teacher, he comes across Dronacharya, the guru of the princes. But Guru Drona turns him away.

The tribe in which he has been born has little access to teaching. Such craving for education enjoys no social support. Drona declines to be Ekalabya's teacher, deferring to the shastras. But this does not dishearten Ekalabya. He does not abandon his efforts, blaming his ill luck. He practices his skill, drawing inspiration from the image of the guru. Slowly and with great patience, Ekalabya enriches himself with skills in archery. But the story described in Ved Vyasa's *Mahabharat* does not end here.

Luckily or unluckily, Drona, the mentor of the Kurus, has an encounter with Ekalabya once again. Ekalabya gives an effective demonstration of his accomplishments and mettle, astonishing Guru Dronacharya. Although an untouchable and outcaste, Ekalabya demonstrates before Dronacharya how through unswerving will power, faith, love and relentless enterprise, a person can transcend the limitations imposed by traditional rules.

The heart of any teacher would exult over this kind of achievement by a disciple. Had Drona possessed the real heart of a teacher, he would have, overwhelmed with joy, embraced Ekalabya. This should have come as a lesson to Dronacharya, the teacher. The mask of convention would have fallen away and the real guru within Dronacharya would have surfaced.

However, the poetic vision of Vyasadeva, the creator of the *Mahabharat* was perhaps lacking in such courage. For the sanctity of human values to supersede social privileges necessitated an audacity, which Vyasadeva did not possess. That is why the courage of Ekalabya appeared to Vyasadeva as mere bravado. And, to punish such unthinking ways, Dronacharya had to resort to some poetic justice, and this brought him low, from his respectable stature of a teacher. Casteism won and aristocracy had its victory, but the stature of the teacher got tarnished.

Consequently, the wise Drona got transformed into an envious Drona. Forgetting the exalted creed of a teacher, he became malicious towards the success of a learner. His ill-will sullied the kindness in his heart, and he set out to deploy his cunning against an unsuspecting disciple.

He asked Ekalabya to present an offering that was due to a teacher in those times. In the Sanskrit language, there is a grammatical link between the words *dakshina* and *dakshinya*. But in the Ekalabya legend, the drama enacted to ask for *dakshina* and the payment of *dakshina* had no place for *dakshinya*. Drona asked for Ekalabya's thumb, and the latter sliced it off and offered it to the teacher.

One wonders what purpose was served by Vyasadeva through this scene. In Indian scripture, the Guru carries the image of a father. Would any father ask for the thumb of his son? Would any father ask for the manhood of his son? The poet or the creative artist, who in his epic got such an unusual story enacted- which culture was he trying to represent! If in the history of any country, in any age, any such custom received social sanction, to what extent can I feel proud calling it mine? To what extent can such an event give me true inspiration to mingle with such a society?

In her version of the story, Annie Besant also intended to provide an interpretation. She said that Ekalabya's story should not be accepted by us as an instance of inhumanity, as there is a philosophical truth latent in it. In her own words, everyone is born according to the thoughts and actions of his past life. Ekalabya's body is also subject to the Karma of his previous life. One should confine oneself within the possibilities specified by one's Karma. It is not the duty of man to transgress such limits out of greed, to obtain more in life than is his due. One must wait. The duty of a good man is to accept such limits as inevitable. Then only can one mitigate one's previous karma, and going ahead would become feasible.

However, Ekalabya lost patience. He had little willingness to wait, and he longed to experience spheres of learning that were denied to him by the restrictions of his previous life. Such efforts got him involved in a sinful act. Only through chastening his body, could he atone for his sins. And in this act of redemption, Drona, acting as facilitator, completed his duty as a guru.

Thus, Truth can be interpreted in very many ways. The interpretation of truth is philosophy. I can accept one such interpretation by Annie Besant. But I do not think she produced this interpretation for high school pupils. Perhaps she would not have liked to impose such spiritual ideas on adolescents in high school. A boy, who is growing in the modern world and is going to accept it as his own, would not be helped by such an interpretation.

The society that believed in casteism also believed in the philosophy of Karma. Man accepted the interpretation of life oriented after Karmavada. Within such a society, Drona was called an Acharya or guru. Whatever the reason, the values based on Karma of that society have now been established as antiquated. In the present climate, our interaction with values of other systems have made us look at our society with differently and we have tried to correct it accordingly. In today's politics, this vision is called democracy. All persons would enjoy the right to have similarity of aspiration as they have been born equal. In the life of the modern man, this has been approved as the most appropriate philosophical interpretation. This might be either Indian or unIndian, but it is the philosophy of today's man. The administrators of education, who, through the story of Ekalabya, are out to educate high school children about religion - are they not dampening children's enthusiasm to wade into the thick of modern life? Let their guardians deliberate over this problem.

These days, many books are being written on the economic and social progress of post-Independent India.

All offer the view that the efforts and the success accruing out of this is not as speedy as it ought to be. The reasons are more than one. But foreign observers point their finger at Hinduism, which they say is responsible for slowing down progress in this country.

The theory of Karma has paralysed this country's limbs. One receives only what has been destined by Karma, and the efforts of man can in no way alter his destiny. Therefore, there is no point in having any such aspiration. Whatever ought to happen would come to pass automatically. Karma would never come to a halt if the Lord so wills. Therefore, leaving everything to His will, we would only embrace Karma. India has been engulfed by such a negative world view. And that impedes the economic and social progress of our country.

If somebody's children study well that is the positive outcome of his *bhagya* (destiny). And if my children are lagging behind in studies, it is because of my adverse destiny. The deplorable life of a destitute by the roadside is the result of his Karma. And if a clever individual has a fleet of cars and is building storey upon storey and can multiply thousands into lakhs, he is just receiving the results of his Karma. Sorrow, suffering, happiness, and wealth are not the creation of man; they are the results of Karma. Man has no role to play in such a situation. He has only to bow down to circumstances.

Our faith in *Karmabada* over ages has rendered us quite indifferent and made us cruel and heartless. Today, we cannot even conceive that it is within man's capacity to build either a good or a bad society - to create glory or ignominy. Applying our will, we can change the society a great deal and can bring an end to injustice or ugliness. We cannot even imagine such things today as we get churned within the whirlpool of the philosophy of Karma. Our capacity to feel gradually becomes blunt. I would like to call the social philosophy of Karma as the cruellest curse laid upon our society.

About five years ago, on my way to Gangotri and Yamunotri, I stayed for a few days in a Sanskrit school in Rishikesh. The age of the students ranged between 10 to 17. One day while offering Arati to the Lord - they chanted a prayer which made me quite depressed. The essence of the prayer in Hindi is that this body is like a mere dry piece of wood and would be blown away by a gust of wind. Therefore, we should pray to the Lord, considering the body and the life inside it as illusory.

In a country, where teenaged children standing at the threshold of life, sing in praise of the unpredictability of life, no good can ever accrue to that country even if God wills it. Shankaracharya called the body a temple and the saints of Odisha called the body the Srikshetra or the abode of Lord. The aspiration of man is not controlled by his doings, his aspiration in fact controls his actions. Ekalabya's aspiration should have controlled his actions. The poetic vision in Mahabharat is only a depiction of his Karmic interpretation of longings and aspiration.

How would those writers, who would compose the Mahabharat in the present age, depict the character of Ekalabya? There are so many young people in India who are deprived of the privilege of education. There are so many youngsters who return rejected from the doorsteps of the Dronacharyas. Such situations are often explained away as normal. Though not called normal, at least they are called inevitable. On the one hand, there are many in our society, who are offered lots of ways and means even if they are neither ready nor prepared. On the other hand, there are many who have no path to tread. They are born poor and are counted as do- nothings.

The agony of their lives become material for literature, which is presented in ornamental language. But such literature cannot fill their stomachs. This literature is unable to offer them admission into any new channel. The omnivores in our society lead lives of lotus-eaters, consuming literature on the destitute. Out of this literature, they try to derive some theory. In the political platforms of this country, dreams, to restore the lot of the destitute and the penniless, are being dispensed. Yet politics has not given any favourable turn to their destiny, as those who manage it have accepted this inequality as normal.

The glory of an Ekalabya would not accrue from only being rejected and being deprived. Those who accepted it lying down, those who own it as their lot, the social or the systemic poverty with the poverty of mind would not find a place in the Mahabharat of today. An Ekalabya can emerge from those who believe that whatever is called tradition is not the only truth and that truth has numerous, changing possibilities. Even though the doors of academics are shut on their faces, they would not be cowed down. Even though the Dronacharyas installed in modern durbars turn them away, they would never bow down to their lot. Their faith in change would remain as firm as ever.

The children of our society these days are quite obstinate and disobedient. This was not the situation years ago. In the golden ages, the junior obeyed the senior, children obeyed their elders, the inexperienced deferred to the accomplished. In schools, pupils accepted their teachers as equal to Brahma, Vishnu, and Maheshwar. Of course, it cannot be affirmed that in those days no one had any dissatisfaction or resentment or behind all obedience lay only devotion or fondness as the only force. It was only fear that saved us from wrongdoing. Even though we were dissatisfied, we complied. Howsoever cruel the teacher might be, the pupil carried out his instruction; compliance was termed social discipline. Previously dissatisfaction did exist, but no one expressed it in so many words. These days, anyone who is dissatisfied has started speaking out. Therefore, whatever is being alleged as disobedience, I would like to call fearlessness.

I will only establish my stupidity if I claim that all those who are disobedient can shine as Ekalabya. Yet, I say they might constitute a group from which some Ekalabya will emerge.

Translated by **Dinesh Prasad Pattanayak**
An essay from 'Ekalabya Katha'

The Essence of Religion

Many scholars and analysts have interpreted and discussed religion using different methods and approaches for which it would be insufficient to merely go by the etymological meaning of the word 'religion' in Latin. Specially during the last hundred years, many committed and uncommitted individuals have discussed 'religion' and given their views. Though unaware of the sense in which the word was used originally, many modern analysts are getting interested in discussions on religion. Scholars and theoreticians, atheists and agnostics are all discussing religion.

Of course, it must be admitted that as a victim of memory loss and delusion, man has created a mass of indigestible ideas and irrelevant sensibilities called religion. Autocratic rulers have often used religion as a convenient weapon. The desire to establish a following or a coterie has at times made religion a victim of earthly temptations. Blinded by such covetousness, we have developed a temptation to enlarge our empire or power instead of having a kingdom of religion. Used as playthings by opportunistic forces, religion has become a means for achieving ignoble ends. Men indulge in sloganeering designed around caste, community, and nation and delude poor and deprived sections of humanity with false assurances regarding religion. Those downtrodden people have been fed with the opium of religion so that forever they remain poor, fearful, and lonely.

Darwin's theory of evolution propounded during the middle of the 19th century has affected all areas of European thinking; it has also more or less influenced religious thinking. It has created within men's minds a kind of all-knowing attitude about religion. Having collected facts and figures about Adivasi societies, anthropologists have laboured hard to discover from them the causes and origin of religion. Religion has been created just by putting a civilized garb over magic, sorcery, and ghost-rituals dominating the primitive societies. There are enough indications to arrive at these conclusions. The primitive man was afraid and considered himself helpless and powerless before nature. Having no power over nature, he fabricated many comforting ways to keep nature satiated. Therefore, many scholars consider fear and helplessness to be the mother of religion. Many also advance the view that man has started imagining religion to exalt our personal and communal necessities to an ideal level.

The interpretations given by psychologists perhaps excite the greatest curiosity. They say that all the desires that crop up in the human mind and all that man creates through religious channels are only meant to gratify one's own dormant or unsatisfied desires. Religiousness is often called an addiction or self -oblivion. Religious practice is called a mental flight. During man's development, religion is taken as an aberration. Many describe religion as a spiritual libido. Many of us perhaps know that European psychologists and mind-scanners have tried to establish that the life of Jesus Christ was only an instance of insanity.

But basically, religion cannot be comprehended by following any one interpretation. Scanning human history, we can realize that when any severe crisis has afflicted human society, religion has given shelter to man, and it has revealed the path to salvation. The noblest of human beings and torchbearers have talked only of religion. These children of humanity have revealed to us the innermost secrets of wisdom. Religion has always come to man as a source of potent support. Religion has greatly inspired us to realize the ultimate truth of life.

A mere transformation of the fears inside man's mind cannot be called religion. The one who frightens us, chases us away. We would like to run away from the people of whom we are afraid. But history would provide ample evidence that religion has never chased man away. Man might have been disconnected from religions, but he has returned to religious path again. He has acknowledged religion as his ultimate shelter. When the world and human society encountered some appalling crisis, holy personalities have called upon human society to return to this path of religion.

We usually conceive life in binary terms while getting distressed with our daily routines. We divide the world into two divisions. We assume the universe to be a strange summation of a thousand contradictions. Mentally we move along a polarized world consisting of good-bad, profit-loss, high-low and above all heaven and hell. Our vision of life gets divided like this. We formulate our opinions according to our likes and dislikes. Afflicted by such a dual vision, we try to pull along in life and end up getting entangled in a network of appalling uncertainties and helplessness. But when, in a calm and collected moment, we take a sober look at life and try to discover our link with the future, we realize we are connected with all these by some invisible thread—not just with the present, we realize we are also connected by that invisible thread with the future. All the divisions of the mind and the consequent fragments disappear. And altogether, there remains a consciousness of the integrated whole. All the names and forms get merged together and melt into each other. With our inner vision we visualize all the currents of consciousness as a part of an undivided mighty ocean. And they emerge from that supreme ocean and again melt away into it.

This transcendent consciousness is inherent in all of us. At the moment of our greatest realization, this has of course given us inspiration. This has never turned down any of our worthwhile quests. The bold onward march of this quest, in course of time, has acquired the name of religion. Efforts have been made to give expressions to the supreme realization, through various terms like 'Truth' and 'Brahma'. The One has continued to exist encompassing the many and it has continued to exist transcending the barriers of time and clime. All has been created but of that One. And that One has given sustenance to all. This declaration of mankind is the boldest of all. This luminous and immortal omnipresent Being is the same being residing in my soul. The ancient seers of India have chanted that mantra. Philosophers have described that One in many names as unborn, primordial, fountain head, among others.

While trying to give a luminous form to religious life, man should not try to mess it up with basic concepts of religion with whatever he had created on earth. Through various institutions like the temple, the church, community, monasteries, the edicts, man has only tried to get closer to that One. Incarnations like Rama, Krishna should be understood as symbols that point to that One! Restricting our devotion to the symbol, we have incurred lots of spiritual losses. Talking away the truth indicated by the symbol we get only a meaningless framework. Without the indwelling truth, the symbol becomes as meaningless as an empty pitcher. Our efforts made with tremendous enthusiasm to display our symbols as different and more glamorous than others, make us lose the truth inside the symbol. We have become as good as insane not trying to understand the total implication of Dharma or Religion, of the symbol pointing to it. Lots of blood have been shed by us and we have introduced ungodly ways to the world. Saint Meister Eckhart, a great spiritual figure of the medieval age Europe has cautioned us about the symbols being mistaken as Truth.

The fullest realization of the Jivatma— the individual soul in the Paramatama or the cosmic spirit— is the basic goal and fundamental message of religion. These words have been expressed in different ways. To rise higher, an individual self feels within itself a spontaneous inspiration. It receives a mission to merge with the cosmic spirit at the purest level of consciousness. Once the human spirit reaches that plane, all doubts fall away. Man becomes composed and discovers his own authentic identity within the verities in the most exalted and ultimate level. The mantras of the Upanishads voice the permanent union with this cosmic soul. In vast ocean of human intuitions, these Upanishads, can be called tiny Upanishads but are nothing less than invaluable gemstones. The prayers in the Upanishads invoke to move man from falsehood into truth, from darkness into light, from death into the deathless. Every person is like an atom and a cosmic atom and within it remains concealed infinity. Every religion has announced its goal to get the limitless within the atom united with the infinite that pervades it. The divinity latent within man must mingle with the divinity of the wholeness of the universe and the Buddhists seers had announced it to be the essence of religion.

Rendering human will lifeless and inert through some psychological hypnosis or physical intoxication, man enjoys a kind of oblivion and ecstasy, but this should never be confused with the realization of the cosmic spirit. Religion is innocent of magic or sorcery. Religion is the realization of the truth of divinity within a complete life. The cyclone caused by sudden pressure or physical symptoms of a filariasis patient cannot be compared with the realization of Dharma. A diseased mind cannot assimilate religious philosophy. In the words of Spinoza, only a healthy man with healthy mind can comprehend religion. When Dharma blows over life like a seasonal wind, when it can permeate all the faculties of life and gets them lifted up, real Dharma becomes possible.

But what are the ways for such a realization? Even though we lock horns over the benefits of these paths, the ground of these paths of history is the same: we must snap all attachments with worldly life and all the nets of bondage must be torn and we have to transcend all the petty limitations of ego and senses. The cravings and desires within us give us the severest of thrashings. They keep our life divided into many bits and pieces. Man can find liberation if he can remain free from these petty and narrow bondages. If we can shut our doors against everything transient and trivial, our doors on the grounds of spirituality would fly open. Once we come in contact with spiritual ground - all areas of our life would become vibrant with spirituality. The momentary world would perish, and we would be reborn in a world of timelessness. The Buddha has called it Niravana, the extinction of the ego. On this ground of Nirvana, the subsequent steps of spiritual life must remain present. In the words of various saints of various religious faiths, we find numerous mentions of this extinction or spiritual death. One who would like to keep himself alive will lose himself. And only one, who would like to lose himself can save himself. This is the statement of Jesus Christ. In the words of Socrates, those who discuss and analyse authentic philosophy are only trying to be close to death. Meister Eckhart has announced that only a person who is altogether dead can enter the kingdom of God. A free man, Spinoza had said, cannot think about anything excluding death.

The goal of religion is a full life. In today's world, things have lost contact with the whole. Life has lost its rhythm. Therefore, religion poses a mighty challenge for the world. In every field of life, we remain paralysed due to various constraints. This situation today is a big challenge for every individual who longs for religion. One might worship any deity in any temple, this challenge of course will knock at his door. One day the empire of religion will be established in the world. Those who believe even today that the Gods' light and love will rule the world, today they have to encounter organised separation, division, and hatred. Their paths are terrible to walk over. The paths of religion are all along impassable like the razor's edge.

The messiah, who embraced the cross, smilingly said "One who is close to me is standing near fire."

Translated by **Dinesh Prasad Pattanayak**

An essay from 'Sila o Salagram'

Sila: Stone; Salagram: Stone collected from the bed of River Ganduki, which Hindus consider a form of Vishnu

Making something our own

When we speak of our own home or the village of our parents, we feel as though we stand firmly on the ground, like a tree anchored to the soil. Similarly, the places where we perceive our roots, we call them our own. The more one claims people and places as one's own, the more fortunate one becomes.

How happy is the farmer who has his own land! Similarly, a person is fortunate in this world if he has a garden surrounding his house, his shed stocked with cattle, a family inhabiting his home. He, who has a present, has a future also. From the present, he can look back to his past. He, who does not have a present, has neither a past nor a future. His life in this world appears meaningless.

You become intimate with persons and things you consider you own, and love them. When you go to the school you own, you never learn there.

During childhood, he who reluctantly listens to good advice, can never internalize those messages. Once he becomes an adult, he discards the learning he was forced to acquire in his childhood. For him, the learning was a shadow which he moves out of and feels relaxed.

To make something you own is remain closely attached to it. When you feel that you are living for somebody else then you live a different kind of life. The wise men live for acquiring knowledge, they make it as part of their being. Similarly, the scientist's love for the cause of science. Scientists never labour in their field expecting any reward or recognition. Ignoring their own happiness and comfort, they search for something unknown. They develop their entire time and energy and feel contented. History is full of such instances from ancient times till today. They make sacrifices, so that world becomes a better place to live in.

A patriot dedicates his life to the country. He never feels the pain that he endures for the country. He feels as if he is coming nearer to his desired goal. If needed, he does not hesitate to sacrifice his life for the country. He never dies rather feels that the country has also recognized his sacrifice.

An idealist lives for this ideals. He does not choose his path under anybody's advice. He never tries to imitate people, whom others consider exemplars. He takes decisions in life not based on calculation of profit and loss, which govern transaction of commodities in the market place. He only loves his ideals, lives with it, and derives pleasure out if it. He feels that his house is always full of happiness.

From our ancient tales, we hear the stories of such persons who loved God. Such people were there in all ages and all countries. They are here too. They feel that the Gods are their most intimate companions. They love him and his creation. They live for the society, seek nothing for themselves and do everything for alleviation of sufferings of the human beings. They never consider anybody. Hatred finds no place in the map of their lives. They consider everyone their own, and feel part of humanity. They have demonstrated in their lives that if you could make God as part of your being, life becomes immensely fulfilling. They remain above all prevailing ideas, faiths, beliefs, religion and seeks, never consider any of these as bad or inferior.

Those who fail to relate themselves with others, do not live for others find themselves struggling in a ditch of their own making—called self-obsession. They are possessed by ghosts called my home, my family, my property, my fame, and glory. Their thoughts and feelings are filled only with poisonous, selfish desires. During their lifetime, they keep themselves engaged in amassing wealth and property. They hate others, other religions, countries, languages and communities. They remain under the illusion that they can be considered eminent only when other appears insignificant. Living in a pond they envy the ocean.

All these people are armed with power. They want only to rule over others. They fear intimacy with another. They do not have a friend in the world, but only try to overpower others in the race of life. They want to enjoy the world alone.

These power-loving people cannot love anything else. They remain busy acquiring sharper weapons of power throughout their lives, but fail in establishing strong and meaningful human relationships. Those who call everything their own become violent, cowardly, and heartless. A coward is an unloving person, he can only excite violence, and cause cruelty to others. A loving person can establish friendship and ensure fearlessness in this world.

Translated by **Sangram Jena**
An essay from 'Satybratara Sanshaya'
SB Publication, Cuttack, 1989

Bhima Bhoi: The Poet of Mahima Dharma

In Bhima Bhoi's poetry Mahima Dharma finds an eloquent and resonant expression. He has enhanced the glory of Mahima Dharma through his literary contributions. He has given poetic shape to the liberating canons of Mahima Dharma and thereby His poetic articulation of Mahima Dharma has immensely enriched our. Bhima Bhoi was Kondha by caste. He was born in a poor tribal family. After his father's death, as per Kondha tradition and due to poverty, Bhima's mother married his uncle. The village of Bhima's birth has yet not been clearly ascertained. Driven by poverty in his childhood, Bhima Bhoi had to move from village to village in search of a livelihood. This may have given rise to the difference of opinion on the exact place of his birth. Taking cows for grazing, Bhima Bhoi earned a meagre amount, which, to some extent, helped his family in getting sustenance. His mother pestled rice and uncle worked as a daily-wage-earner in households to maintain the family.

While watching cows graze, Bhima Bhoi used to sing in the company of cowherd boys. Gradually he started composing his own songs and sang them. At that time he was composing folk songs. In those days, the tales centred on Radha and Krishna along with Gopis were narrated to entertain the masses. Bhima Bhoi used such stories in his early writings for composing his songs.

Bhima Bhoi had probably encountered the spiritual teachings of Mahima Gosain when he tended the cows as a young boy. "There is no casteism in society. Everyone is born of divine glory-" must have touched his heart. These words might have filled his hopeless heart with rays of hope. He might have internalized such words of enlightenment and preached among his people with abundant enthusiasm.

There is a legend that Bhima Bhoi fell inside a well while following the herd. While trapped inside the well, Bhima prayed to Mahima Gosain with consecrated heart and soul. Impressed with Bhima's unfailing faith, Mahima Gosain came to the spot and rescued Bhima from the well. It was at this time that Bhima's poetic genius blossomed. Being commanded by the Guru, Bhima had gone to Joranda settlement. There, after receiving the instruction to preach the words of the Guru in own poetic form to his people, he came back to Rairakhol. Later, he left Rairakhol for neighbouring Sonepur, Gadajat, Binaka, Buluda, and Bhusapalli. Moving about these areas, Bhima Bhoi reached Khaliapalli and finally settled there. Bhima Bhoi breathed his last as a householder monk. The memorial temple, carrying his mortal remains, still exists in Khaliapalli.

The palm leaf manuscripts of Bhima Bhoi have been preserved in Khaliapalli. Some of the manuscripts have appeared for public view in printed form, like *Stuti Chintamani, Nirveda Sadhan, Brahma Nirupana Gita, Adiyanta Gita,* and *Srutinisedha Gita.* Two other unpublished manuscripts are *Mahima Binoda* and *Manusabha Mandal.* The first of the two has been written in Bengali-Odia and the second is written in Sanskrit-Odia. Besides these, there are other palm leaf manuscripts like *Ashtabakra Gita, Kaliyuga Gita, Jashobanta Mahamandal, Mahima Gopana Bhabisyata Malika* etc. There are numerous Bhajanas and Jananas written by Bhima Bhoi. He has written 'Chautisa' and 'Olata Chautisa' too.

In the prime of his life, Bhima Bhoi had written 'Rasarkeli', 'Jaiphula', 'Dalkhai', and 'Baulagita'. During that period, Baishnab Kirtans were being composed in the Bengali language. Under their influence Bhima Bhoi might possibly have written *Mahima Binoda* to entertain his followers. It is a voluminous manuscript. More facts about Bhima Bhoi's life would come to light once it is published. There are some Bengali bhajanas attributed to Bhima Bhoi. He might have written the Bengali songs for recital by his Bengali devotees or else he might have composed those songs to illustrate their affinity with Bengali kirtan, extremely popular at that time.

Manusabhamandala, a book written in a language in which Odia mixed with Bengali probably has a different background. It should be recalled— some books whose authorship is ascribed to Panchasakhas— have been written partially in Sanskrit. The Bramhins at that time had alleged that the Panchasakha poets wrote in Odia, as they did not have knowledge of Sanskrit. In order to prove them wrong, the Panchasakha poets ~~have~~ incorporated some Sanskrit lines in their Odia books. The tradition of writing books by saints in these lines might have continued till Bhima Bhoi's time. And this might have inspired Bhima Bhoi to write at least one book in Odia with some sentences in Sanskrit which was *Manusabhamandala.*

Bhima Bhoi's poetic works might have been derived from two major sources. One has been acknowledged by Bhima Bhoi himself- blessings or compassion of his guru Mahima Gosain. It is said, Bhima Bhoi had accepted his guru's command to put up at one place and exercise his creativity, instead of moving about in propagating the dharma. The other source of his poetic creation is his sense of empathy. Right from his birth, he had been troubled by the vagaries of life so deeply that he could not forget those feelings even after he embraced a spiritual order. Rather, those experiences brought his spiritual insight closer to real life. A devotee dedicates his life to the Lord with devotion. An inward empathy becomes the chief trait of a devotee. That becomes the base. The devotee becomes a saint on that ground. He becomes a poet and draws his inner experience very close to life. This empathy had drawn Bhima Bhoi's language closer to life through an evolutionary process. In other words, while searching for a proper medium, Bhima Bhoi could get his own language for expressing his empathetic feelings with lively ease.

Bhima Bhoi's poetic inspiration came directly from the source to which he had dedicated all that he had. One who correlates directly to the Perfect Person realising him in his inner self and walks keeping pace with him, gains his vision with perfect touch and masters his poetic skill. Two hundred years prior to Bhim Bhoi's time, there was RITI yuga(age) in Odia literature. In order to excel in poetic skill of that age, the men of letters memorised the *Amara Kosha* [The Thesaurus by Amar Singh]. They worked hard to prepare dictionaries of their own to be comprehensible to the readers. It was a prevalent practice those days. But Bhima Bhoi's style was more accessible to ordinary people.

If one opens up through someone's inspirational touch, all his untold inner emotions are released through poetry, through the companionship of the saints, through living life beautifully. Like all other saints of the world, Bhima Bhoi's life is a pertinent illustration. Whatever Bhima Bhoi has written, is not a show of scholarship but an exposition of his roots. It is inborn and an original identity. It issues from the primal root so intensely that it appeals to all of us. As readers we are intimately touched by Bhoi's writings.

Bhima Bhoi has not looked for and chosen the words for writing his poetry. Words have come to him spontaneously on their own when he sat down to write poetry. He declares:

"My poetic skill owes its origin

To the compassion of Sriguru

I am too young an urchin

I have no wisdom of my own";

In one of his Bhajanas he has openly stated that letters cannot be set if His compassion is not there. Another poem (Chautisha) embodies the following popular lines,

"I compose poems in haste,

I do not know the beginning or the end.

Vedic or Non-Vedic,

Oh! Lord of these three worlds

I put down it for your perusal"

Again in another bhajan he writes:

"Listen everyone

He gave me the poetic skill

And himself roams about the world

Bhima the unprotected states

That can never be forgotten"

Accepting all these as his crowning glory and linking his poetic skill, Bhima Bhoi states metaphorically in his masterpiece:

Do not blame me as I have posed as a poet in the world

The world is full of guile, lust and gain, vice and discord.

How shall I spend my days in this world of injustice and illusion

You have tied my body to the world

With the three strands: Firm triguna.

Showing creation and arousing desire

You make me restless here.

[*Stuti Chintamani* Ch: 34]

Bhima Bhoi has placed Alekha at the highest pedestal for whom he displays his poetic skill. In a Bhajana he defined Alekha: "People couldn't write about Him for ages and named Him Alekha, which means unimaginable, indescribable, and immeasurable.

The saints realise the Bramha in themselves. Firstly, they search it outside. They enter the world with experience. With the wealth of their inner being they make whole of all the fragments. Those who first begin with the exteriors they try to locate it with the scriptures, scholarship and outer worship and they may be able to assess it gradually. But in most cases due to fundamental indifference or disgust they withdraw themselves inward. External renunciation propels them to seek themselves inwardly in the isolated field. They become saints and renounce the world. They become mystics and label the world as illusion. The man who tries to enter in his self, snapping all the strains, reduces the intrinsic faith in himself to some extent. The ways of the saints are otherwise. Realising the internal experience a saint spreads from within to the outside world. As he is related to God inwardly, he comes out easily and correlates with the outer creation of God. He snaps illusion of all sorts with faith and fulfils all the wants with love. With the song of faith, he denounces all the fears.

Bhima Bhoi is the poet of Bramha realisation. He is the poet of this world filled with Bramha. Having reposed faith in human world he is the poet of Man. His realisation of Bramha drew him closer to suffering humanity. There are few instances of poetic expression of such empathy in Odia literature, perhaps even in world literature. As a being of flesh and blood who came from the lowest rung of the human society, he had to suffer all sorts of woes like a common man deprived of minimum sustenance. Having personally experienced sorrow and deprivation, he could realise the suffering of humanity at large. His spiritual realisation did not drag him into his own self alienating from the world. He came into the world with that realisation and became immeasurably empathetic. He wished liberation of beings and prayed for the liberation of the world. Bhima Bhoi engaged himself with the type of penance that a saint practises and receives the desired boon, thereby fulfilment. In a passionate prayer for the universe Bhima Bhoi sings :

"Where shall I hide, how shall I live
And escape by which way?
How much shall I record the sufferings and danger
That would come upon the earth by the way ?
I have surrendered my body and the world
At the feet of Alekha the lord
I am pleading for the whole world
In His presence now
Where shall I live if the limitless world
Will be drowned
This body and the world shocked me deeply
If this world of men is annihilated
Where shall I move about?
For that reason, I pray to the Lord all the while
On the guru, concentrate.
In hundred eighteen couplets
Bhima Bhoi prays with tears-overflowing eyes."

[*Stuti Chintamani*]

One who is in the body is in the world too. On that account the body seeks the world, gets restless for the world. The penance that confines the self with attendant excitement and misery and intends to snap all relationship with the world, might not have realised the identity of the world with the body. So the saint deems it his primary duty to pray for the world before the Lord:

"The twenty one abodes are coming to an end

Rush in and hold up my lord the world is falling into deep pit

Lead the boat of pity to rescue it

Hold up the earth and shake it up

Otherwise it will sink and be lost

Don't blame me later as I wouldn't

Let you know where the earth drowned"

[Stuti Chintamani]

Again at the end the world-famous immortal couplet -

"The infinite misery of humanity

I find unbearable

May my soul be consigned to hell

For the redemption of mankind" (x x)

[*Stuti Chintamani*]

Translated by **Dr Satyananda Swain**

An essay from 'Dekhu Dekhu Keba Sahu'

(How can one bear human misery)

Looking at Vivekananda anew

If we were to go to back to the India of a hundred years ago, we would see Vivekananda at the forefront of all the distinguished people around. He had pondered deeply over the various problems facing India and had also come out with solutions to these. He had indeed seen ancient Indian education from a new perspective, and had provided a much-needed dynamism to the stagnation engulfing the education system. At that time, as per Indian tradition, those who were renouncing the world to embrace sainthood, they kept themselves aloof from the complexities of life . They considered life as futile and insignificant, and to be one at the divine feet of the Lord, as supreme mokshya or freedom from the cycle of life. But Swami Vivekanada was of a different mould. Only a sanyasi, a man free from desire or greed can show the way by being at the forefront of life. And through his life and deeds, Swami Vivekananda led by example.

After Swami Vivekanada India has witnessed many an upheaval in these past hundred years. Because of its contact and clash with the West, a Renaissance changed Indian society in manifold ways. Indian literature also saw the emergence of a new era. But what is more significant is that from such a renaissance was born the aspiration for a political freedom movement, and after passing through several stages, it did achieve freedom and independence from colonial rule. Swami Vivekanada was not in politics. He said on many occasions that a sanyasi should always stay away from politics. But he never considered political servitude and dependence as one of the causes responsible for the decline that India had witnessed on several fronts. While contemplating on the ways India could be freed from the manifold chains, he had never ever paid attention to this political angle. Maybe then, time was not ripe for the advent of such a moment. Still, when the moment came, an attempt was made to free the country from servitude, and then Vivekananda became a source of inspiration for many to achieve the desired goal.

It sounds strange and astonishing that Swamiji's words, spoken hundred years ago, are still very relevant. Possibly there is some pertinent message here, an enduring appeal of life that never ever gets old. Or, even when old, these messages are manifest before us with a new form and that is why we cannot dismiss these messages as obsolete or old. And there is such vitality in these messages, that with every passing year, we realise their importance. Keeping all these in mind it seems as if Swami Vivekananda is still with us, walking by our side. Not just as a teacher or a guide, but as a companion, and hence he does not seem to be old-fashioned. Ideas, when they become obsolete, just dropdown and fall on the way , and you don't worry about that. They remain as just things of the past, as a part of history. But here in our country , while walking down the road of life , Swami Vivekanada on many occasions comes and reveals himself before us , and sometimes we feel like judging ourselves by making him our ideal, and wishing to know what happened in the then India to those hopes and aspirations that he had for India .

During the subsequent decades the struggle for India's political independence became the prime goal and endeavour. Perhaps it was all preordained and accordingly, leadership was also prepared. Still then, the leaders of the freedom movement promised to translate those dreams Swami Vivekanada had seen for Indian society and people, into reality, and that promise inspired the most. That there would be no caste discrimination, and everyone would get back his dignity, that there would be no poverty, and there would not be any oppression of the marginalized by the upper class people, that the government based on fear would come to an end—all these promises instilled hope and confidence in the minds of the people . New means were devised for the struggle for freedom. Alongside political independence, there was always this concern to bring social transformation. Independence came ; Indians became citizens of an independent country; people got equal rights as per the Indian constitution ; and accordingly some bills were also passed. But what happened after that?

Fifty years after independence it seems as if the desired vehicle for change has halted somewhere on the way. In independent India crores of rupees were spent on new constructions and human development , but discriminations between high and low remained; hatred kept people apart. People were dishonoured before their countrymen. People in power stayed as the only capable ones ; fear and uncertainty intensified ; and what to speak of a new education! The educated ones became more violent and primitive , as if they had resolved not to listen to their conscience. True, the gentle and polite, to cover what they lacked within them, moved around speaking about environmental pollution. But deep within them there was something toxic and obnoxious. In their wickedness, they crossed all limits. The one occupied the seat for which he was not qualified; one pretended to be someone he was not and was eloquent about issues for which he was not fit to speak about and boasted as if he was the sole custodian of truth. The courageous and the brave became weak and cowardly. Hence people in large numbers became sycophants and achieved their ends through flattery. This country fell came under the spell of neo- feudalism, which put on the garb of royalty.

Religion was not capable of providing leadership. It was absolutely difficult to decipher the appeal of spirituality generally linked with religion as in many cases it attempted to survive by compromising with people in power. During the nineteenth century those religious people who had made tireless efforts to shape the collective life of India with the help of the magic touchstone of spirituality, they were worshipped as gods, as heroes, but they were forgotten. They were preserved as pillars in the museum of Indian nationalism, as if they were pieces of treasure. What more, Swami Vivekananda came to be treated by some as if he were an antique piece bought from some market. Some insignificant sects claimed him as their own; and some false Hindus wished to use him as a royal witness. The brotherhood of men once created by Swami Vivekananda, and the one he had succeeded in keeping with Sri Ramakrishna's blessings, ultimately embraced a lonely sojourn. The fear that Swami Vivekananda was tarnishing Sri Ramakrishna's legacy by bringing in ideas from the West, gained ground among many. As a result that said forum appeared as a sect among the many sects present. That Sri Ramakrishna Mission had a distinct say on different problems of India was never felt again. The idea brought home to all and sundry by Swamiji that spirituality had the power to help people face the manifold challenges facing the world became has lost its potency. The places where there were establishments of Sri Ramakrishna and Swami Vivekananda attracted the devotees like temples, but these failed as centres of inspiration. It was as if, to preserve Swamiji's inheritance perfectly and wholly in a house once built by him became very difficult for want of sufficient space.

Swami Vivekananda had once expressed the wish that he would always be born in India till hunger and fast are there. Perhaps it is not true that he was telling like this because of some deep attachment on his part for India. He protested against such a system and was not prepared to tolerate why a man who has come to the world with God's intention and his essence should not be able to satisfy his hunger and live amidst constant afflictions and inadequacies. He fought and rebelled against such a system where society and its attendant financial role force men to live in misery and helplessness. Swamiji was able to declare with courage and conviction that for the rise of any sense of spirituality, you need to solve the clamour for food for the belly. And for that so many religions, and the luxury of many a prayer are to wait , and give way for the solution of this foremost inadequacy. It is not true that he was disrespecting his teacher when he said that even Sri Ramakrishna Paramahansa is to wait. Possibly one can justly say that Swami Vivekananda said these words to bring to the limelight Ramakrishna Paramahansa's words of wisdom. This means that he emphasized that the first step should fall first. Swamiji wanted everyone to realize that religion and spirituality had a distinct role in shaping each and every man. And maybe because of that he laughed away the desire and longing of realising the harmonious contact with the God in heaven through individual liberation to be extremely selfish and unspiritual. He wanted such a society to be established where there would be no special privilege or opportunity, and it means that because some people would enjoy everything, others should not be deprived of anything. There would not be any exploitation. After a hundred years , one feels like believing that if India's saints, instead of delivering empty sweet nectareous words from those false pedestals , would have paid attention and listened to the words of Swamiji, then at present India would have kept its reputation as a powerful spiritual country in all the world, intact. If a just and rightful step had been taken in uplifting the people after getting political independence, India would not have looked so dull and lack-lustre.

In independent India, if spirituality had been assigned its due place in matters of political leadership, it would have served as an inspiration for the entire world. The country would not have suffered from the stagnation and sloth that have gripped people from the core after independence. Religions would have led from the front; they would have spoken courageously about gods, justice and the rise of spiritual powers; they would also have warned the kings and their politics to follow their religions and by doing that they would have influenced them to follow the right path. Sure the numbers of muths and hermitages would be more in independent India, compared to the ones during Swamiji's time. The number of saints would have also increased accordingly. Nowadays, the number of pravachaks, or spiritual gurus have increased manifold, maybe because of the rise of God-fearing people. But how come none among them speaks like Swami Vivekananda! Even, someone has not ventured to open his mouth to instil fearlessness among the people in India. As if they are being rewarded by the people in power, all of them have more or less compromised themselves, and they do not saying anything to challenge the current establishment. Because of so many reasons, they have lost their power, and so they have no option save walking within their confined circles. It seems as if Indian spirituality is passing through a poor phase. Swami Vivekananda was only Swami Vivekananda in the beginning, and that is why, even when he was attached to a particular community, he had given this exemplary account of a unique identity. When someone has experienced something, and is somebody, even when he is in a community, he is not tied to it. Nowadays the spiritual persons possibly are helplessly bound to their sphere of communal ignorance. It is because individually, they have not experienced any spiritual encounters in their lives.

In India, must poverty, starvation, humiliation and indifference cover the lives of the poor and the deprived? Should they not try to find new ways to usher changes in their lives? After nearly a hundred years of Swami Vivekananda's death, one wishes to ask that question first. In India, as Swamiji wished, so long as some thousands or lakhs of unmarried youths and sanyasis, who have forsaken their homes, have not come forward to volunteer for humanitarian service and education, darkness of ignorance, starvation and humiliation will be their lot. To bring to light and manifest the divinity hidden within you is true religion, Swami Vivekananda used to say, and the revelation of the innate humanity of man is the primary purpose of education. Here in this country, it seems people as if they have frozen. Even if they are products of a a cruel social system and even when born in a land of affluence and possibilities like India, they live the life of pigs, and they never ever think that there could be an alternative way to escape the stagnation surrounding them. And who can tell them with full conviction that divinity is within them? And accordingly , this land awaits the imminent arrival of a leader who would come and say that someday our humanity would open a window, and become stronger by getting into a free world , and that leadership would not wait for the *sanyasis* to wake them up from their slumber. Who knows, leadership may stem from the political domain, or, unexpectedly from a completely different field!

One who realises this truth would not keep himself tied to a groove. One who would be feeling directly that there would be a complete transformation of man during the coming evolution, he would be the medium for the new consciousness to flourish. What with the happenings in the world around, the traditional structures too would collapse and break down to pieces in India. The true rebel, the traveller on the righteous spiritual path would not be bogged down by such structures. From within him he would get the direction from his guru, and hence he would not be tied down to the discipline of a school like a sheep tethered to a pole. One who gets the message from within is reckoned as a guru by the world, and he does not give up anything, or even, he does not struggle against falsehood. In the process of living with the truth, he embraces falsehood and transforms it by a unique expansive process in the heart itself. Even when he is looking up into the sky, he does not snap his ties with the earth , or, when he is thus tied to the earth by many a string , he does not cry saying that he has lost his touch with the sky. He does not renounce the world in order to change it. He lives in the world more intimately and with so much of affection than ordinary people. Like God, he constantly looks after his people. Because he loves the world, he fights against darkness, indifference inequality, and apathy. To do that he does not declare himself as a hero or a master; rather he lives with his people as a friend. Swami Vivekananda possibly never had the desire to be a hero. Those who never wanted to change themselves and were making uproar to be his disciples, only those had made a hero out of him, and as if being driven by their own compulsions, they tried to keep him under their spell.

Swamiji was talking about such a desired path as the path of Vedanta. As per the Indian tradition, the meaning attributed to Vedanta is conditioned by a specific regional appeal. Because of that when people hear that word in the discourses of Swamiji, many Indians become elated. At one time Vivekananda had speculated that Vedanta would be the religion of the people in our world, and keeping that in mind, he had delivered a lecture in America. Because America had a democratic form of government, he said so many times that it would embrace Vedanta as a way of life. Here in fact he has not said anything about Vedanta as inscribed in books. Swamiji held that Vedanta manifests itself here in our world when it is governed by a relationship where everybody sees God in every man or material being, and discovers the new intimacy created thus by such a realization. Now the truth that is only sealed in the books of the philosophers would be revealed to everybody. If Vedanta becomes the way of life in India, then there would not be any class enjoying special privileges, and there would not be any distance or discrimination between man and man. The feudal system would go away, and people would move ahead, embrace a new brotherhood. People would no longer live separately in our contemporary world, tied to their specific grooves or cultures, believing half-truths as their religion, philosophy or God. Now, being inspired by this new continent of humanity, those island-like sects would open up and integrate with others.

And, the process of translating this new possibility would begin from the ground, from this granary, this primal land. Spirituality would not be imposed on men from above like a superstructure. Earlier, religions with their imposed structures of rituals have very much weakened men. By creating an exaggerated view of afterlife, they have kept people in the dark about today's world. As a consequence, the world itself has become very weak. The real world would carry in its fold all men and move step by step. So from a new expression would be created men's economics, his politics, and his society, and spirituality would be at the core of such endeavours. One that is described by Swamiji as the stage of child's play of all religions, is gradually losing its appeal and more and more people are becoming free from its bad influence. For past is what lies stagnant, what separates and what shelters distance. Because of that unrule, there would be no space for someone in economics, politics or even in social life. A new free road would be open as per one's nature and there would also be equal opportunity for the overall development for all. That is why there would not be any question to swallow anyone in the name of religion or any other path.

Swami Vivekananda has described India in glorious terms for all of us. The land is also a symbol; we make our land glorious because we are committed to it. Or, to tell it in clear terms, by making the land a medium or a base, we as a community would take oath to build and live our life for a greater cause. To judge it from this perspective, in our nationalistic sentiment there is hidden in disguise a stimulus for spirituality, which, when we so wish, link us with a higher life. It is not that because we are born to a particular land, that land is sacred and glorious. What matters is we, tied in so many threads of intimacy, stay closer and committed to our land , and maybe , here lies the truth and propriety of such a bonding. Swami Vivekananda had dedicated himself to the cause of India. He had stayed committed to this land. He wanted to take this country to a lofty height where, it would serve as an beacon of spiritual unity. And that unity will lead us along the path of prosperity.

If you move further and further on the path of commitment, our country would appear to us as our motherland, and we cannot think of ourselves as otherwise except as sons of our beloved motherland. There at our home our mother rears us, nourishes us, accords us distinct identities, serves as an anchor in various spheres of life, and because of that she seems to be our own. And because she is our own, to us she appears uniquely beautiful. We grow up, wheresoever we become somebodies, or earn anything, because we have dedicated ourselves to our country. Whatever Swami Vivekananda had said, he had done that from India itself. To make India vibrant and prosperous in all respects, he drew inspiration from all corners of the world. He had dreamt of building the mansion of his desires here in India itself and for that he had expressed his wish to use his time in a very dynamic and enlightened way. After a hundred years whenever we think about Swami Vivekananda we feel as if his dreams and the desires are manifest before our eyes. And for the sake of India one is driven to become more committed. When we are able to serve people, it would seem to us as if Swami Vivekananda is our close companion. Whatever challenges he faced hundred years ago in India and always dedicated his life and kept it open , even now those challenges are before us and are still calling us. And, if anyone agrees and shows a slight interest in responding to those challenges, and tries to listen to those calls, we feel as if Swami Vivekananda is present physically and is walking with us. Would such a path ever end?

With such a commitment Swami Vivekananda also tried to discover India's rich past. As much as we feel and experience our present fully, our past also would reveal itself before us accordingly. There are some who would like to run away from the present to somewhere else. They accept the past as a shelter; during the past century all those intellectuals who had spoken about India's luminous past, were very active in the present. That is why they never showed any interest to take shelter in any ideal cave of the past. They tried to look for sparks of inspiration in the past. By gathering the necessary sparks from the past they attempted to get a proper perspective of the present. In contemporary India there are many who cannot manage the present or have profited from the bad deeds of the past, and try to project an inflated view of India's past. May be out of extreme enthusiasm or extreme shrewdness they constantly give us the bad advice to return to the past. Swami Vivekananda had never said anything supporting such people. He has never become enchanted or tired by looking at the past. Rather he had always tried to gather the sparks from the past. Whatever he has chosen, he had expressed it in a new way by giving it the name of Vedanta. He has thought of Vedanta not for India only but for the whole world as a religion of the future.

Translated by **Kalidas Misra**
An essay from '*Bhinna Janey Vivekananda*'

A Portrait of Tribal Culture

We, the non-tribals who talk about the tribals, are often easily discernible from them. As a deer is dear to a hunter and cheers him, as a tamed tigress remains an object of affection for the owner's fancy, as the guinea pigs are liked by elite scientists engaged in serious scientific investigation, probably in the same way, most of us are fond of tribals.

In the words of Verrier Elwin, we study the tribals, at the most, with a museum interest, and with the same interest, we love them too. We never wish to be one amongst them. We always consider it wise to maintain a safe distance from them, as we are scared to be intimate. Howsoever deep our attraction for tribals and their culture, it only goes to the extent, which is very touchingly put by Laxmi Narayan Sahoo in his poem 'The Natural Man', *"but you must be above, below, must be the other"*.

Tribal culture is a complete culture. In the 19th Century, a European researcher on culture had referred to tribal people as the 'Dusk Race' or the 'Night Race'. It was not surprising that he had considered Europeans as the 'Day Race'. In India, we, the non-tribals, sometimes think of the tribals in the same way. It is blind belief, rather ego-driven blind belief. Tribal culture is not at all a simple culture –howsoever diminutive or uncomplicated it may seem from outside; it possesses diversity and breadth. Tribal consciousness is perhaps comparatively less widespread in comparison to our modern life consciousness. But it has more than one historical determinant.

The tribal society, in other words, is said to be a primitive society. Many times, the isolationist critics of developed societies wield the word 'primitive' with derogatory intent. The reality is that the tribal society is perhaps a less mobile society. In that sense, we may categorize it as primitive. It can be argued that tribal society is a closed society and symbolizes stagnancy. Yet, inside its boundary, each tribal society has its own economy, polity with conventional rules and regulations. And as an appendix to it, there are also different religious beliefs, worshipping and propitiation practices, songs and dances, ecstasy, and guilt consciousness. Unitary tribal societies are small; relationships and interactions are quite local, and therefore, instantaneous. The technology used in everyday tribal life is also rudimentary. The complex division of labour, which is the hallmark of a modern society, is never seen in a tribal society. A tribal doesn't change his environment; rather his environment is a beacon that sets the direction for his actions. A tribal accepts himself as part and parcel of the nature that surrounds him. Therefore, a tribal doesn't desire to conquer nature, rather he considers living within the boundaries of nature and in harmony with its inhabitants.

The paradise of a tribal lies on this earth. All his sorrows, perception, and emotions are regulated by an animistic sacredness. Therefore, his experience of divinity is not at all controlled by any elusive hedonistic detachment. It is possibly only in the tribal culture that one finds the direct expression of the well-articulated life-view as presented in "The idea of the Holy" by German critic Rudolf Otto. In the terrestrial faith of the tribal almost everything is direct, perceptible, and hence lively. If any culture remains fundamentally symbolic, life in such culture manifests itself in all its richness and grandeur.

In tribal society and culture, concept of "the individual" does not exist; in fact, such a concept has not been born. It is the community, which is the only all-important and all determining authority in their society. But in that collectiveness and its authority, we do not find the extremism and oppression of modern collectivism of various shades. In such a scenario, we discover a kind of participation. In the universe of tribal culture, the umbilical cord of the individual attached to the society remains intact till his demise. The extent of weaning in society that could endanger the individual has not occurred in tribal societies. It is, at once, the charm and the handicap of the tribal society. A society always provides an individual a wider field for movement; a society moves forward through individuals' lives; all kinds of new changes become possible. It is for this reason alone that we can detect vibrant ideas of collectiveness in every kind of imagination in a tribal society, from its meadows to its universe of thoughts, as though individualism is taboo.

In a tribal society, an individual has certain assigned roles; a sense of individualism is almost absent. Man becomes artificial when he alienates himself. Upon deliberately accepting artificiality, perhaps he rises, step by step, and acquires confidence to do something new. But in a tribal society, there exists no individual divorced from the community. Hence, the entire mutuality in their society has its origin, probably, in the unconscious, which causes plain fellow feeling without any hue or characteristic. To move away from the bind of the collectiveness of the community life is the greatest disaster for a tribal man. For him, social death is more miserable than bodily death. What modern alienation means in the so-called civilized society has no relevance in a tribal society.

In Indian scriptures the tribals have been described as forest dwellers. Everywhere in the world, the tribal groups dwell inside the forest areas. This, however, should not be the reason to conclude that the tribals always lived in the forests. In the African sub-continent, which was once known as Dark Continent, the archaeologists have also discovered many proofs about the existence of prosperous ancient civilizations. Before the Aryan influx into India, the non-Aryan tribals were not at all forest dwellers; they had their own country, polity, and administration. They were displaced by the Aryan invaders and became forest dwellers. The Aryans appropriated their religion, culture, and lifestyle. The entities, which tribals held in their imagination as of some value and consequence, were embellished with Aryan dress and definition and gradually came to be identified as Aryan Gods. Lord Jagannath of Odisha is perhaps a manifestation of this process. Those who have captured Lord Jagannath through such appropriation see this process as a confluence. But in this process, those who have been deprived still feel deceived.

Poverty is the most common feature of tribal societies worldwide. It is as though the tribal has accepted life as nothing but "to endure". That tribals have remained naïve over the ages is a misconception prevalent in the non-tribal society. Are they not naïve, when, upon being asked, they would even cut off their fingers? Should it be termed as naivety, endurance, or a self-inflicting helplessness? In India, out of every 100, seven are tribal, whereas in Odisha it is 23. In our state (Odisha), we find 62 different tribal communities, which constitute half a crore population. In the state, there are at least three districts, where the tribal population is higher in proportion to the non-tribal population. Almost 97 percent of the tribals live in rural areas or in forest areas. The rest three percent, the so-called city dwellers, as reported, live marginalized in city slums. According to the 1971 census, while the percentage of literates in Odisha was 26 percent, the literacy among tribal people was even less than 10 percent. In case of women, this percentage remained at 2.5 percent. If the textbook measures and definitions of below poverty line (BPL) are applied, then 99 out of 100 tribals live below it. The irony is that they still live in a condition in which they were living perhaps 500 years back, yet they have remained extremely indifferent. In the reckoning of many of us, they are yet to be considered as human beings. Even they consider themselves almost as jungle trees or mountain stones.

The non-tribals go to the tribals with a sense of superiority and a feeling of guardianship, which in the words of the anthropologist Knoebar is an "ethnocentrism of the benign kind". They go to them to show sympathy. It is a superstition that is prevalent in Indian culture that sympathy to the poor enables one to reap the fruits of holy deeds. In Indian tradition, sympathy has been conceptualised so atrociously that in it there is no place for fellow-feeling and the feeling of being one with the poor. In our world, the well accepted attitude of the civilized human beings towards the disadvantaged tribals, as has been in vogue, is what the noted anthropologist Malinowski has said, "discriminative give and invidious take". While discussing Indian literature and culture, we, most of the times, remember the tribals with meaningless emotion. It is a kind of ill-inspired emotion, which is synonymous with 'worthless earnestness', the term coined by Karl Marx. Such emotion, howsoever innocent it may appear, is nothing short of barbarism.

Almost with this kind of barbarism, we have brought the tribals into our literature, danced their dances in the capital city and collected their folk songs. We feel immensely elated and gratified in bringing these things to the corridors of civilized society. We also feel relieved. This is escapism; an eagerness which gives us a lot of consolation, amnesia, and a feeling of attainment, particularly when our surrounding and present appear to have become defunct. Through this, we have perhaps raised our glory, and managed to hide our real faces under masks. But no gain has come to the tribals. The obscurity in which they were living continues. Humiliation at the hands of non-tribals continue to be their lot, and their economic poverty has made this humiliation eternal.

The society, where many plans and programmes are designed expecting change in tribal societies, should allow leadership to emerge from within the tribal communities. This has neither occurred in Odisha nor in India. We, the non-tribal lords, have made up our minds to get richer by pushing tribals deeper into poverty. We, the non-tribals, have gone as teachers to teach the tribals. We teach them to remain subordinate to us through ridiculous imitations and by losing their self-respect. We impose on them our models, and, in a very crude way, we throw them into our pits. In the political arena, we have placed fetters around their legs. With all our good intentions, we have started destroying their foundations.

The real growth and development of tribal people is possible only by tribal leadership, never by the feudal lords. The day, on which a tribal can speak on his own about his culture and its past and future, a truthful description of the tribals will be available. Those home-returned tribals, who we have taught to remain as our tamed elephants and trained to dance in streets and official functions, also cannot provide real leadership to the tribals. So, the real process is neither showing them sympathy nor trapping them in forms of slavery; the real process is their conscientization. This is the process to begin looking at tribals not as tribals but as human beings. This is a process to create a dynamic and throbbing conscience so that the tribals do not feel like human beings.

According to Evans Pritchard, an anthropologist, we enable ourselves to understand our own society and culture in a wider perspective only if we delve deeper into other societies and the culture. It is only then that in the background of a larger human experience and social life, we understand ourselves more completely and realistically. Perhaps this is a useful principle to study tribal society and culture and determine its real self. Those who we have vanquished we treat in a self-serving and arrogant manner, neglecting them as unkempt aborigines. We have held such neglect as our privilege. The more we, the non-tribals, inspired by true fellow feelings, move close to the tribal society, the more we study and learn from it and get benefited, the better we can understand ourselves as human beings, the better we can live genuinely connected to our tradition. It is only then that the misfortune of small fish being devoured by bigger ones and forest dwellers being devoured by city dwellers can be averted. It is only then that true social harmony will be achieved in India.

Translated by **Anjali Sahoo**
and **Birendra Nayak**
An essay from 'Odisha O Odia'

Existentialism: Towards a Vision of Life

Every man in this world has an innate awareness of his elemental kinship with fellow human beings and feels lonely when deprived of this sense of kinship. To fill up the void caused by separation, man resorts to subterfuge. He erects different kinds of fences around his life and dons the garb of varied ideologies just to hide from himself. Yet, the burden from life's load continues to weigh him down. And then he sulks, cries to himself, cries against the world, and hurls countless allegations against it. These allegations gnaw at and eventually cut the cord that connects him with the outside world. While facing these unresolved questions, a few who profess to be intellectuals weave a net of logic around their existence to understand it better. They call this net of logic existentialism. With existentialism as their framework, they evaluate life.

However, logic does not help one to get rid of the burden of life. However zealously one views his life from the perspective of any philosophical concept or ideology, one doesn't succeed in being freed of this burden. As long as existentialism prods us to escape from life, we cannot realize the fundamental nature of existence and the significance of life. To find the real roots of existence, we have to search our lives in a larger context. The spheres of our individual lives are encased within larger spheres. Only by expanding our narrow selves to these ever-expanding widening spheres, we can realize the true significance of our lives. There is a vast infinite sky before us. But we must make an inward journey and plumb the depths of our existence to experience the infiniteness of this sky. Only then can we find the real roots of our existence. Then, a spontaneous intimacy, not the seduction of intellect, becomes the quintessence of our lives. Our outlook then becomes life-affirming.

Existentialism has a history. At first, this history dwelt with attempts of the intellectuals to conceptualize existentialism and then to understand human existence from the canons of this concept. But soon it outgrew this limited intellectual approach to understand existence and sought for an idea of existence as it continuously evolved through love and acceptance of life. This history had a chronology of evolution in the Western consciousness. In contrast to how existentialism pervaded the West, it was imported to our country. There were people in our country who had read European literature and drawn inspiration from it. They defined their lives according to the postulates laid by existentialists in the West and proclaimed themselves as modern. They brought the idea and style of existentialism into our literature. As these people also ruled over our literary world, this alien, imported style was also imposed on our literature. In course of time we, the laity, began to accept Western existentialism as our own. This country also has its own history, its own way of life. Independent of the European trend, our literature could have had its own chapter on existentialism, which was neither borrowed nor implanted but rooted in our culture and history.

Existence is eternal; existentialism came in much later. Much before the idea of existentialism, man had pondered over his existence from many perspectives. Through diverse traditions, man had always surrendered himself to the society or to a superior entity. A life of surrender was always a simple life without any worry or tension. But at the same time, it was also a life of smallness. The traditional man had always been a small man. He lived in a small, confined circle. Owing allegiance to the society or the traditions he built a system of ideals and truth for himself, and he lived a contented life within that system. But with the advent of modern science, the walls of that sacred system collapsed. A spirit of scientific enquiry broke his illusions and made him self-conscious. He, without any external influence, began to examine his own life and the world around him. He discovered the centre of his existence within himself and began re-evaluating his own life. He noticed and rebelled against the discrepancies between his inner self and his outer world. On the one side, he himself and on the other, the collective of religion, tradition, society and the like with their visible and invisible fetters trying to lead him onto a predetermined track— he began to view his existence through a new critical perspective. He began to realize that these fetters had kept him dependent and impotent, in subjugation and slavery. Religion, ethics, nationalism, economics and politics had made him live like a puppet. In course of time, it dawned on him that he really didn't have any stake in all these clever games of the powerful; rather everything had been unjustly thrust upon him. He craved for independence from all these visible and invisible fetters. The blossoming of democracy and the expansion of universal education in Europe instilled in him a new sense of being as a free individual.

There was a dichotomy between what an individual with his inner longings wanted to pursue and what he was forced or pressurized to do by societal or traditional values. He experienced a kind of existential dilemma in this dichotomy. This brought him loneliness and a feeling of emptiness. The period of two world wars in Europe and the communist nightmare in Russia sowed more doubt, dread, and angst in his life. This was the first phase of existentialism. But this also led to a period of protest, seeking new meanings, and discarding old definitions and institutions. From this churning, the second phase of existentialism emerged. The latter led the first phase of existentialist discourse into a wider circle of a newly refreshed humanism. Right from the 15th century, with the upheavals of the European renaissance, the foundation of humanism was continually being laid. But these were in an abstract and nebulous form, waiting to take concrete shape. Towards mid 20th century, as the colonies were being emancipated in Europe, for the first time in its history, the rest of the world became visible with each nation having a new identity of its own. This led to a discernible evolution of the human consciousness. Earlier Europe was accustomed to believing that it was the centre of the world. Europe believed that only her literature, philosophy, science, and culture was of significance. It viewed people outside of Europe as mere commodities. But now, considering them as equals, Europe desired their company. This paradigm-shift reset the relations among different nations and a new perception of reality emerged.

With this new perspective, it was not proper to sulk at life, at the world and flee from it. With this new humanistic vision, we had to look at all human beings around us and confront the crisis of our existence in a spirit of togetherness.

We had to go beyond our loneliness. Then only this world would be like a home for everybody, and life would seem no more as a burden but as a door. Through that door we could enter and become friends with all the people of the world, moving past the stage of loneliness in which we had erected fences around our small individual lives. The discourse of existentialism now embraced the shared destiny of all human beings. The individual freed from the shackles of his ego merged himself with humanity. It happened not only due to external pressures, but because the individual experienced an ecstasy in merging his life with that of his fellow humans.

At the very beginning, Marxism had proclaimed every individual as a member of the human society. But later, this liberal life-view of Marxism was used just as an expedient instrument of politics and an effective means to gain power by communist governments. The atrocities committed by the Russian government after the communist revolution could not be accepted by the existentialists. The premise of an individual's existence was not just political, but fundamentally human. This premise began to encompass politics and economics and provided a fresh way of evaluating power and authority. Existentialist literature intended to ensconce man in that all-encompassing premise. It intended to lay bare all the falsities and half-truths that the individual or the society indulged in earlier. A liberated and energized man– no more bowing down before the authority but confronting it on equal terms, no more fleeing the dilemmas of life but facing them head on– tried to find the meaning of existence in the symbiotic relationship between his own life and the life of the larger society. Existentialism came to be defined by these values.

Such awareness opened new vistas in psychology, psychoanalysis, religious discourse, literature, and art. Existentialist discourse tried to broaden itself in sync with the widening spheres of man's existence. Existentialism became liberal and inclusive, to be committed to all life in a spirit of love. It had already experienced in the last three or four decades that when we looked at life only through our intellect, we were confronted with loneliness and a sense of emptiness. People were living like outsiders to their own lives and tried to escape from it. But existentialism, as it evolved, gave rise to a new love and zest for life. It awakened new possibilities in man and in the world in which he lived. The elemental longing for life's fullness brought new dimensions in his response to power and authority. It assured him of an alternative path amid the collapse of hope and faith.

When the weak fences that men had built around their houses crumbled and narrow ideologies collapsed before the surge of a humanistic conscience, there were still some people who clung to their ideologies. To assert their identities, they fought against other ideologies; but all of them, in the process, fell by the roadside. The basic ideas of Gandhian and Marxian ideologies were assimilated into a universal credo of humanism that had found acceptance, but some people preferred to remain in their Gandhian and Marxian cocoons. This obduracy was also seen in some existentialists. They were not able to see the woods for the trees because they were engaged in petty ideological battles with others. However, existentialist discourse evolved to be the torch bearer of a universal conscience and was ready to meet the challenges of human existence.

We can discern this trend in the humanism phase of the existentialist discourse, beginning from Carl Jaspers to Paul Tillich and then to Martin Buber and Victor Frankl. These men spoke of faith in a world where faith had dried up. They spoke of emotions in a world which had been spiritually famished by the rule of intellect. When cowardly leaders, fearful of losing power, armed themselves with terrible weapons and proudly called it statecraft, existentialism propounded the idea of 'courage to be'. When an atomized society made people lonely, the existentialist philosophers brought in the idea of dialogue. They spoke of 'will to meaning' to a people overwhelmed with the emptiness of life. These insights led man from a life of illusions and artifices to an authentic life of love and fulfilment. Man is no more cynically resigned to his existence. There are now blossoming signs of love and acceptance of life. Modern science also has renounced its traditional scepticism and has now begun to speak of new illuminating dimensions of human existence. Bound by our ego and confined to our shells, we were not able to appreciate the full possibilities of our lives. But now the life-urges of the modern man, enlightened by a feeling of universal love, are veering towards the realization of these possibilities. This idea of universal humanism is finding greater acceptance among the people of the world. How would we like to view this development—an idealistic stance or a pragmatic approach to life? Or is it a synergy of both in a new dynamic of universal empathy?

Meanwhile, the powerful, clad in the cloaks of nationalistic or any other ideology, have become more savage. Who will win this war? Will it be possible for us, who desire to live life in its authenticity and beauty, to halt cruel powers? But one thing is certain— those of us who still remain sceptical of the sun that has begun to brighten the horizon will soon move past our scepticism and step into the broadening vistas of life.

Translated by **Jayant K. Biswal**

An essay from ''Sukara O Socrates' (Socrates and the pig)

Orissa and Odia

The word "Orissa" refers to a geographical piece of land, while the word "Odia" is the name of a people as well as their language. The language has its own literature, which possesses a unifying trait. Are we, only the ones who speak the language, to be called Odia? Are those, who live in this province speaking different languages, to be also called Odia? Since ancient times, not all the people staying in this land only spoke in Odia. Numerous tribal tongues flourished before and along with the Odia language, many continue to exist even today.

The name of the land, Orissa, is also relatively recent. To be precise, the Moguls, coined the name Orissa for the coastal tracts to the south of Bengal that they acquired. When the Moguls were establishing their hold over the coastline, other Odia speaking princely states called the Gadajats also existed. Before the arrival of the Moguls, different kingdoms that covered roughly the same territories were referred to as Kalinga, Utkalinga, Koshal, and Toshali. Kings fought among themselves, each trying to prove his kingdom's deities more glorious than that of the rival. Rulers,who managed to conquer three or more contiguous kingdoms within this geography, declared themselves sovereign of the entire Kalinga. But they came from further down south. These were not wars between different groups of people; the wars can be understood as contests between rival dynasties to establish sovereignty over a somewhat homogenous population in terms of religion and culture.

We began thinking and referring to ourselves as one people only after nationalism permeated Orissa during the last part of the nineteenth century. Odia nationalism gave rise to the emergence of a different kind of leadership in this land that had no parallels in the past. Thereafter, the literature being produced in this territory was stamped as Odia literature. We saw a convention called Utkal Sammilanni. However, we must bear in mind that the people who led these conventions, campaigns, and social movements were concerned with keeping only Orissa's Odia speaking people in the forefront. The programme to establish an independent province of Orissa, uniting all the Odia speaking people in contiguous provinces of the time beyond the borders of Orissa's political division, began at that time. This nationalistic fervour at the time was so one-sided and single-minded that perhaps our leaders did not think of the other people who lived in these territories but spoke other languages. The latter were assigned a place outside the emerging mainstream.

As Odia nationalism was gathering momentum, the larger movement for India's independence encountered this relatively local project. Some leaders were more invested in Orissa's political goals than they were in the national movement. Doubts and differences arose. A leadership emerged that intended to create a channel where local and national resistance to colonial rule could be merged. Sometimes, leaders of movements remained confined to their immediate goals. A few key figures in the Odia nationalism movement began to feel that Indian nationalism was a threat to Odia identity or Utkaliyata. They had already conceptualised a unified Orissa as their nation and feared their goal may be devoured by the larger Indian nationalism project. These leaders thought their local aspirations would remain safe if they kept their ambitions confined. However, another set of leaders aspired to go beyond the narrow and the familiar to the wider sphere of Indianness. This conflict refused to die for a long time. Two personalities, Pyarimohan Acharya and Gopabandhu Das, worked hard to expand Odia nationalism's horizons. It is probably easy to grasp the challenges and possibilities of those times through the conflicts and crises faced by these two people.

Anyone who does not wish to be pointlessly sentimental, must quite readily agree that Orissa should mean all its people. When leaders from Orissa demand resources and funds from the Centre projecting Orissa as an underdeveloped state, they seem to have forgotten that even today there exists wide disparity between regions within the state. No plan of action has been worked out in Orissa taking its entire people into consideration– whether it is the economy, culture, or education. Odias who enjoy high status look down upon the rest. Even if Odia language is accepted as a cord of unity in Orissa's communal life, the distance between elites and non-elites persists. The elite class of people in Orissa are embarrassed about conversing in Odia. Consequentially, ordinary Odias, almost as a rule, continue to always consider those high up as strange and remote. The distance between the people privileged to receive an education and the people deprived of it is perhaps greatest in Orissa in comparison to all other states in India. Orissa was created as a state so that the people who lived here could lead their lives in an accepted unison. But how can collective unity be possible when a few people are turning into big fishes that see the many as small fishes and believe in devouring them?

Orissa would have been different today had we been able to think differently. Orissa has considerable natural resources, people with great talents; we also enhoy the foundation of a continuous civilisation and culture, we have our literature, music, dance, and architecture. Despite having all this, why are Odias from different strata of society unable to lead an ecumenical life? Even though our elders have wilfully ignored the problem, let the new generation think of it again. Notwithstanding their education, those who do not wish to remain detached and exclusive from the illiterate masses, let them come out of their narrow existence and try to establish intimacy and kinship with as many as possible. Then they can surely forge a different kind of Orissa.

Once, Europe also underwent this age of nationalism. But their national awakening slowly expanded into an all-human awakening. The early emergence of nationalism paved the way for many other political and social developments. Nationalism erased feudalism in Europe. Ordinary people also found spaces in all kinds of nation-building projects. Education was made universal, social systems were suitably renovated, and every individual experienced some degree of inclusion. Fatalism departed and people developed self-respect.

In Orissa, we have a long way to go to prioritise such changes. Many people here have not yet found a favourable atmosphere to consider themselves Odias. The Odia, as a people, remain only in records. Where all the people ought to have had a natural self-respect due to their Odia identity, we find that a few people have remained arrogant and ego-centric. They are unable to feel confident in themselves unless they see others as inferior. The knowledge of the erudite among us is unable to serve the interests of all. It is almost as though knowledge aids the learned in only multiplying individual pride. And what is even more strange is that people who are in the ablest positions in our system never find it unbearable to see Orissa, despite its possibilities, remain unhappy and unfortunate. Perhaps they have become like aliens in their own homes.

Speaking in a public meeting, Utkalamani Gopabandhu Das had once declared that people are human beings first, then Indians, and then Odia. It would have required considerable courage to express such an opinion during the height of Odia nationalism. But the moment we start to think about the real meaning of our Odia identity, we shall realize what he had said is true. Once Sri Aurobindo said, one who knows only Krishna does not in fact know Krishna. Similarly, one who knows only Orissa deprives himself from the possibility of knowing others and becoming an Odia in the true sense. We ought to be able to turn ourselves into such perceptive centres that more frontiers appear before us. We will be truly able to see our own perimeter if we can see it in the context of other greater perimeters.

Translated by **Santosh K Mishra**

An essay from 'Orissa O Odia'

An Introduction to Devotional Saint Literature

Adoration is a matter of feeling. In the *Shreemad Bhagavad Gita,* three modes of nature that modulate the passion and action of men have been discussed; all these are the causes of attachment and hence of bondage. We relate 'satwa' with happiness and knowledge, 'rajas' with actions and 'tamas' with various negative emotions such as sloth or idleness. One must exceed these three modes of nature— which implies that they have to be modulated by something higher in breadth and depth, such as adoration and devotion. In the Gita, this is called Undeviating Bhakti Yoga. Bhakti alone can help transcend the limitations of 'Jnana' and 'Karma' and enter the status of Brahma. In 'Sandilya Bhakti Sutra', the 'jiva' attaining Brahma is called proper liberation (Jivanam Brahmabhabaparti multih iti).

In the ways of Bhakti, as the state of adoration without emotion can be imagined, similarly Jnana as well as Karma may remain in a state where there is no emotion. If Jnana does not contain emotion, it becomes a mere cultivation of scripture that breeds fruitless arrogance leading to poverty of knowledge. If Karma does not contain emotion, it gives rise to various excitements, becomes inclined to treading into others' field, making noise, but still pervades man's life like a net. When emotion is blended with action it becomes elevated to the status of knowledge. When emotion percolates through Jnana it overcomes the blunder of self-confinement. In 'Narad Bhaktisutra' various analyses of devotion attempt to acquaint with the emotional content of consciousness. It is said that the experience of devotion of the aspirant makes him mad-like, stunned and God-like (Matta bhabati, Stabdha-bhavati, Atma-Rama bhabati.) Without right emotion none can become outright mad and stunned, or outright eager and steadfast in faith, let alone become God-like in status. The one whom man has been searching eagerly becomes the essence of his experience, which gives him the plenitude of God-like status. Even after that eagerness lingers and subsequently gets settled permanently, though the roots of it are twined with the supreme existence which is inherently the part of our being. In truth, whatever we search outside and passionately try to experience in the outer world is ingrained within us in our being. If its presence were not felt inside, the eagerness for its quest in the outside world never would have been felt. One who gets its touch on the outside first and becomes eager by its touch, the same eagerness connects him with that plenitude and source of which remain within; it puts an end to his quest, stuns and the roots of the aspiration enter the earth it needed. One who gets its touch within first, becomes stunned and searches for it in the identity with all eagerness and turns his objects of belief into identity which implies that he assesses everything with the help of his findings within. Whatever makes it possible is nothing but adoration. The Bhakta, who is the adorer, connects the supreme principle of life with his inner and outer living and offers all his life to it. Whenever he misses the connection in the slightest manner it makes him perplexed. In the 'Narad Bhakti Sutra' this is how the principle of devotion is described: Naradastu tadarpita khilacharata tadbismarane para- byakulateti.», 19th Sutra.

In another place in the same book devotion is described as: Sa tu karma jnana yogebhyah api adhikatara. It also describes Bhakti as the outcome of Jnana and karma (Phalarupatwat). In Bhakti, jnana does reach its supreme fruition and it also leads Karma to reach its end which brings salvation. It bridges the gap between the inner and outer life.

Without emotive content, knowledge is merely a collection of information. In one religious scripture, in fourteenth century England, it is told that such accumulation of information breeds pride and it admonishes the quest for the desired which must rely only on experience. Adoration and emotive experience cannot leave us in illusion. That scriptural knowledge breeds pride is amply proven taking instances from the lives of the learned ones from history. The experts in scripture, who lack emotional experience make fuss of their limited attainment, claim that they have got enough, write books to flaunt their knowledge, but stop midway as they exhaust all their gains then and there. If knowledge is entwined with emotion, it saves them from such predicaments, their reservoir of eagerness does not go dry, their quest never ends, and their paths do not terminate. The feeling that more path remains to be traversed saves one from being passionate about a lot many ambitions. So long as the circle of emotive experience keeps expanding, the ardour of love never dies, and the core of quest does not get removed from one's eye; emotion gives rise to gratitude, which always inspires one for self-offering that keeps one's multitudinous works connected with one's devotional life.

Spiritual practice involves two methods, 'Utsarpini' and 'absarpini'. The former implies the practice of going upwards from below. He imagines his object of quest abiding in heaven. Probably this has led man to imagine God's abode to be beyond various worlds– he has imagined heaven as Baikuntha. He has perceived that when a man dies, he moves upward to stay in different worlds as the result of his action or Karma. In the scripture of our yoga and tantra, similar ascending spiritual practice has been laid down. The eternal truth has been described in the image of a reverse tree, for which spiritual practice is known as reverse practice. The 'Kayasadhaks' in India make their body tough as 'Bajra' so that it becomes more useful for ascending to the source of their realisation. Practices of such a category are called ascending practices. But those who considered such practice as arduous, adopted the other one known as the descending method of practice. In the descending method of practice, if the practitioner feels it difficult to rise higher and higher by the dint of his practice, he adopts the method of devolution. Man alone does not ascend to God, God also descends to man. Man seeks eternal truth, seeks God, similarly God also seeks man. If man could ascend to God by the dint of his own strength, it would make him more passionate and egoist. Man has meagre strength for which he could never ascend to Him who is mightier than the mightiest; he needs His grace. Such assumption has led to the perception of the descent of God and the coming of Avatar. In eighteenth century, the metaphysician Söeren Kierkegaard wrote "when one loves another, if the former stands at a greater height than the later, he feels the natural urge to help uplift the other to his own height or he may also feel the impulsion to come down to the level of the person as an expression of his love. The same happens in the case of the relationship between man and the divine". Kierkegaard calls such dual mode love as its inherent dynamism. In the practice of adoration such duality in mode remains which implies the process of ascending to complement each other. An aspirant must ascend higher to be closer to it. Whatever remains to be higher and beyond always breeds in man an indomitable eagerness to reach there and on the contrary, the Being there also feels compassion for the individual below to descend to his level. Thus, one mode coexists with the other.

So sadhana, that is, spiritual practice involves ascending on one hand and descending on the other–probably, the basic things in it is one path having two dimensions, two catalysts. Very often, the path of Jnana and the path of Karma follow one of the two dimensions, rely too much on it and consequently become deprived of the plenitude that Sadhana could offer. Even if it comes closer to it, it fails to attain the goal, because most likely it relies too much on its own strength and capacity when an inner quest as well as desire for unveiling becomes the foremost devotion in the life of the practitioner, comes plasticity which prepare him naturally and most agreeably for meeting with the Divine. Knowledge alone fails to bring plasticity and the same happens in the case of sheer action. When knowledge and action are complemented by devotion, only then it materializes. The Sadhak appears not only to be progressing but also coming nearer to his cherished goal which brings natural joy. Whatever the Sadhaka has fixed as his descent that supports him to walk the path, that which makes him eager also is felt to be drawing nearer to him. That is how both the ends provide impetus to bridge the gap and the distance seems to be eliminating rapidly.

In practice by adoration all over the world one gets to learn how both move even enthusiastically towards each other eternally. To be with God implies to meet God, to meet Him halfway. Various realisations of the devotee have been perceived as meeting God halfway. He is drawn towards God. Similarly, God is also drawn towards him. Each pulls the other. The history of Bhakti is the history of mutual pulling, it is the history of natural love. The fundamental aspect of its history is that one who thirsts for God from such a great distance is the one also desired by God, because he inherits a speck of Him which is the cause of bond between the two and also because of this the Absolute enters the individual existence in a spirit of kinship. The one searches for the Absolute and the Absolute also with equal eagerness wants to inhabit the one. Such eagerness breeds kinship which results in nearness and bonding. Whoever is one seeking and proceeding to meet, the same takes place from the other side in a way of reciprocation. It begets tremendous faith as if on the other side of the closed door, He is there. The moment the door opens one meets Him; neither the adherer of Jnana nor that of Karma could dare to imagine it. But in matters of Bhakti such a story prevails all over the world.

In the fourteenth century, a mystic Sir Meister Eckhart said the same thing that as we could not stay without seeking God, he cannot stay without us. It can go to such an extent that if we turn our face away from Him, He cannot do the same. Among all religions, Christianity preached this philosophy more ardently. It treats the conception of His omnipotence equally as His image of all–kindness. Not only in India, but all over the world where religious practice is centred around establishing identity with God, the relation between the devotee and the Divine has culminated into a personal intimacy and mostly it has been imagined as a matter of mutual dependence.

Followers of the path of knowledge rely exclusively on their own strength which lead them into the doctrine of Mayavad illusionism. In their pursuit of the Absolute, they annihilate the relative; in their quest for the perfect they annihilate the imperfect, calling it immoral and redundant or devise some way or the other to repress them. They look down upon the world of senses so that they could cherish the world beyond. Such an ideology and practice makes them split personalities. They fight against the darker side that exists within themselves, are wounded and ultimately defeated to plunge into remorse and stay there self-exiled. They have a notion that they have to choose the one between *Vidya* and *Avidya* and so try to deduce that by accepting one, one had to leave the other; but the path of the adorer is different as it involves surrendering all of one's effort and practice to the adored and the sustainer. The path of *Bhakti* rightly implies one need not be induced by self-castigating attitude to repress the senses and desires. Instead of taking them as bondage or fighting with them, one should offer all his sensations and feelings, desires, and instincts to God. One could offer oneself to Him to bring oneself to the right path. It means that one should neither sever oneself from sensory experiences nor refuse their role in life. One has to admit them in life but should not use them for small fulfilments now and then but can use them in the cosmic play to derive delight and contentment. We should not deprive ourselves from varied experiences that the world offers us; experiences open doors to the Divine. This is the way of *Bhakti,* path of adoration and love. God is not a castle that can be captured by the strength of knowledge and power of Karma. God can be won by kinship; through kinship we can offer everything that is in us, so that all our predicaments would vanish and we become ourselves as our friend and then everything would appear very easy and He would undertake whatever is to be done. This is devotion; it is faith and kinship.

The learned follow various theories and principles laid down in scriptures and out of them develop some kind of reasonable solution to equip them to realise God. But the devotee becomes worthy of meeting his God only by nurturing kinship. It is his strength. By kinship, one establishes a bond of love. When one establishes a bond of love, the far becomes near; the sky high above appears to be a reflection on the mirror within, as it descends to the level where one can touch. When it gets reflected in the heart, however at a distance, it does not seem so. When one feels it to be near, faith grows bold; Whoever one intends to reach, it appears to be very close, the bond of love grows. In the scriptures of *Bhakti*, instances of various relationships are mentioned. In the Vedas the *Rishis* who nurtured the element of faith addressed the Absolute as father (*Pitanoasi, Pitanobodhi*). In the fifth canto of the Mahabharat, in the *Narayaniya* section, God is addressed both as father and mother. During the middle-ages in India, Kabir of Bhakti cult has addressed God as mother and himself as child (*Hari janani mai balak tera*). Tulsidas in *'Ramcharitmanas'* says that as a mother protects a child so also God protects a devotee (*Jimi balak rakhai mahtari)*. In Christianity, God is taken to be the father of the Universe; one who loves this world, absolves the sinner from his sin and all his play here is meant to pave the way of man to Him.

First comes devotion, which gives rise to longing for the object of devotion; longing gives rise to sense of kinship which further gives rise to the sense of nearness and then follows a sense of identity. Such is the ground on which all activities can be built up. At first, the devotee feels attraction for his desired deity from a distance and in subsequent stages as he grows up, he progresses to cross all the distance to establish an identity with Him. He lives by that identity; his knowledge comes from it. Identity gives him the opportunity of Truth-awareness and keeps him involved in multitudinous tasks in life. He makes his adoration grow deeper and more intense for the object of his adoration and that divinises his life and he offers himself for the cause of this world. The whole world seems to be his home and all activities in this world become his joyous offering to the Divine. He exceeds all the differences between holy and unholy as well as divine and undivine. That is why in the '*Narad Bhakti Sutra*' of ancient India, it is told that wherever Bhakti goes it forms a place of pilgrimage, whatever he does is pious work, whatever he writes becomes sacred scripture. In true Bhakti-yoga true knowledge is attained and true deed is done; nothing remains forsaken. Sense of identification eliminates various kinds of distances.

In Yoga Vasistha Ramayana, it is mentioned that without becoming Vishnu, if one worships Vishnu, the fruit of worship does not yield to the worshipper. By becoming Vishnu when one worships Vishnu, one becomes worthy of MahaVishnu. In 'Bhabisya Puran' it is also advised that without becoming Rudra when one worships Rudra or meditates on Rudra, the worshipper does not attain any 'Siddhi', which implies that one cannot ascend to the level of Rudra without initially becoming Rudra. It is no sign of pride. In the path of devotion, one cannot simultaneously retain pride and move to his desired end. Devotion implies elimination of distance and a gradual progress to attain nearness with the deity. While worshipping Shiva, gradually the knots within open one after another when ultimately the worshipper becomes 'That' to utter the Mantra "Shivoham, Shivoham", the most logical consequence of the process.

Devotion refers fundamentally to the matters of faith. Behind faith there is inflexible and steady assertion, a consent that never wavers in any situation. Such faith might have evolved from doubts, various quests, and reasonable questions. Once it reaches the conclusive state, it defies all debates, nor also does it give any argument in support of his side. "To have faith means offering oneself and not having any intention of seeking anything. To have faith means to forgive everything, and not to intend to draw conclusions based on arithmetic calculations. To have faith means to remain connected and earnest and not to brood over what might or might not be the consequence. 'Narad Bhakti Sutra' talks about '*phala rupatvat*' which means that by trying to understand devotion and by living it, one can get into its dynamics completely. It implies that the outcome of devotion is devotion alone. It is also the outcome of work, knowledge, and Yoga in their individual perception. Devotion unfolds the deepest aspiration in man to its universal oneness without which both work, and knowledge remain partial, resulting in various kinds of ignorance and improper action. So long as devotion does not rise to that level, it remains shrunk in sheer emotionalism, and guided by intolerance gives rise to multitude of narrowness and atrocity.

The true character of devotion is self-awareness. In the impassiveness of our life, faith and devotion work like the catalysts that permeates into various domains quite naturally and stall a sense of defeatist and petty attitude.

Devotion brings plasticity which makes man more receptive and sensitive. From this point of view, it appears devotion is more daring and accessible than knowledge and work. When knowledge mingles with faith, knowledge becomes the cause of infusing lyricism into relationships. Faith enhances emotional courage and faith added to work drives out dullness from work. That's why in religious practice, devotion has been more inspiring for writing poetry than knowledge. Poetry has generated music. Devotion is our life; it has made all our relationships plastic. Amid diversity and many faceted character of life, devotion contributes profusely to bring the feeling of oneness among many.

From the point of worship by individuals, devotion has matured and become expansive to impact the attitude towards life as a whole. Albert Schwritzers, a humanist metaphysician-devotee writing in the twentieth century, viewed his ultimate analysis of life as 'faith in life'. The phrase carries a sense of humility with an inspirational dedication towards the world. When faith brings man to God it always brings the world to him. He feels as though one with universal life, as if he is tied to it all around. He feels the presence of God everywhere, and as if the destiny of the world is nothing but fulfilment of His will. Such realisation leads him to determine his course of action; he lives for the world and makes himself more and more worthy for the betterment of this world which he accepts as 'Summu bonum' of his Sadhana, religious practice, '*Sarba Lokahite Ratah*', offering oneself for the betterment of the humanity becomes his native religion. He keeps the world in the forefront and remains in the background. He offers to sink himself in hell but prays for everyone to be happy and the world to be redeemed. It makes him more active and consecrated. Reaching this stage, he cannot keep his worship limited to precincts of a temple or an idol. In every form he feels His presence and his worship extends to every form and image. In the history of humanity, those who have been acknowledged as great devotees have also been mighty social workers having effected major positive changes in the world— making knowledge powerful and soulful.

Translated by **Janmejay Dwivedi**
An excerpt from 'Santha' (Bhakti) Sahitya

The Omnipresent Babus

However hard one may try; it is impossible to avoid encountering these babus. They are to be found at all times and in all countries. They have survived in all geographies, from flood-prone areas to flood-free areas, and from the villages to the cities. While they are usually found working within the government, they also manage to thrive outside it. Their names are regularly published in newspapers, while their photographs are featured on boundary walls and books. Some, waiting for the day their names come to the public's attention, carefully preserve their photographs. There are babus who mercifully deign to retire, but there are others who are unwilling.

Babus take life very easy, but they make life very difficult for others. They believe everything is possible if one has intelligence, everything can be said if one has a mouth. They gaze at the world through an attic window, seeing the multidimensionality of life in a single dimension. They make life and all kinds of lived relations very complex, while turning the obsolete functional. They have a vice-like grip over the system. When a system is established, these babus preside over the ceremony ushering in its arrival. When the same system is demolished, these babus— with garlands of flowers around their neck— reserve the specially designed seats around the altar of dissolution. The names of these babus— inscribed on the foundation stones of the temples— shine brighter than the deities in the temples they inaugurate.

If you have tried becoming a babu, you must have learnt something about their identity. After all, while anointing our foreheads with a mark of distinction, we gain some idea about the sandal paste used. When we try to be like others, we get a taste of who they are.

When you become a babu, you enjoy such a deep sense of security that it feels like you are back in your mother's lap. All of life's troubles recede from the horizon. You lead a life of comfort. You construct a building in the state capital and stay there. Then, you sit in the meetings, take part in community feasts, and enjoy the trappings of power. You can enter the world of literature and immediately find yourself among the learned. You can set foot in the worlds of music and acting. You might feel like the controller of everyone's destiny. All your memories of stumbling in life will receive a quiet burial, while you enjoy the privilege of being cremated in Satichaura.

Once you become a babu, it can even settle your caste position. Even if you have no friends in this world, all will come prepared to help you. On occasion, they will probably remain prepared beforehand. They will send your file to the higher officers and, if required, will themselves carry it. Any time you enter an office, the peons, clerks, officials, and non-officials will leap to their feet to convey their respect. From ration-shop owners to bus conductors, all will be ready to give you passage. The moment you dial your phone, your pending work will be instantly completed. You will be worshipped as a Brahmin in our new society. You will be considered God incarnated as man. According to the new varna system gradually emerging after independence, the four varnas of the earlier era have been replaced by two. One is Brahmin, the other is Shudra. If you are on the side of the Brahman, you will occupy a position so high that nobody can reach you. Even without the sacred thread looped over your shoulder, you can easily pass for a Brahmin. Without sitting in a meeting, you can get your work done; even without contesting in an election you yourself can win it.

You can become a lecturer and an educationist. You can decide how many schools and colleges will be opened next year. You will start accepting your place of work to be an extension of your own luck and use that accordingly. You will remain ever cheerful, ever bright. You have at the tip of your finger all the detailed information about what had happened in Europe, what happened in Amaravati, and what happened in the conferences in Chandigarh or Chandipur you had gone to attend. You can explicate and embellish whatever you wish to say; you can even impress the blind by showing daydreams in the dark.

Once you have become a babu, nobody will oppose your desire to become a lecturer, or even reader or professor. This miserable situation has come to pass because teachers and educators themselves do not know how they accidentally got into this profession. They teach, but they never talk about teaching among themselves. The zeal and curiosity of a newcomer will dash against their hard selves and shatter into pieces. The youth will perish and get lost. Lecturers, getting into that trap, develop thick skins and become stagnant. Their students, too, also lose their faith.

O Babu, you could practise literature and enhance the

reputation of your mother and motherland. You, of course, know that literature is a profession open to all. Be you a lawyer, an officer, a priest, or an escapist it does not matter, you can practice exotic literature, can enjoy literature, and make others enjoy it. It does not matter which attire you wear in that world, from which river or pond you drink water, or in which shed you are tethered as a heifer; it should have no bearing on your practice of literature. But these democratic and egalitarian principles have no relation with the literature that prevails in the world of babus. According to them, literature can be taken up as a special addiction or intoxication. Only if the story of their life's upward surge blooms through language, it turns into literature.

If you are a babu interested in literature, you can use literature as a mode of entertainment. You can soak literature with flavours of life; nobody will bother to ask you which flavour you have experienced. You could, through poetry on human suffering, make readers' hearts cry. Though escape-from-life is your supreme religion, you can be a realist in your literature. Though a conservative at heart, you can be a poet of revolution, or you can form an association of revolutionary poets. Though you never change, you can hail the inevitability of change through your literature. You can paint dishonesty as honesty.

Babu, you can easily join a religious crowd or procession while still looking distinct. You can be the chairman of the reception committee of the mega–conferences or mega festivals of religion and religiosity, you can host special lunches or dinners for the invited delegates, and the religious conferences would bless you. You won't have to do anything to gain this blessing. The great minds of those religions will be at your doorstep.

Saints will spend the night at your home, perform *homa*— the holy invocation by fire— to appease the stars. Along with pictures of their divine figures, you will also adorn the pages of newspapers. It is from your house that offerings in the biggest tray will come for the deity and the names of your dynasty will be inscribed on the conch.

President Kennedy said in his address at a university that those in positions of power controlling the destiny of people must admit, along with other things, the truth that we all will eventually die. Kennedy spoke of death only a few months before his own. Babus never believe in this eternal truth. Perhaps no babu has ever cherished in his mind such a weak and unmanly thought, until it is time to face death. I say this because if the babu had believed that we, along with him, must one day die, then how could he have buried for himself mountains of gold and silver? If the babu starts believing that one day all of us must die, then he will descend to the ground from his pedestal. He will share his life with ours and derive pleasure from that. He will probably unbutton that stiff collar and sit easy!

Yes, these babus must die. Leaving them behind is the only way to advance. The shells of this babudom must crumble. The manliness, smothered due to babudom thus far, will emerge one day. That moment is coming.

Translated by **Guru Charan Behera**
An essay from 'Jatire Mu Jabana'
(I am a Shudra by caste)

To Which Gods?

The national character of Indians is showing signs of decay. Writers who consider themselves helpless seek the protection of political masters and coteries after political power was strengthened at the expense of cultural leadership at the national level. Piteous groans issue from the hearts of ordinary people when literature and culture, which are meant to elevate human spirit to higher levels of awareness, surrender themselves at the feet of ministers. Where are you gone, oh gods? Show us a way out of this crisis.

Man does not seek happiness. He also does not want power. He wants perfection and a sense of fulfilment. We look for meaning in the varied experiences we go through. Man cannot find fulfilment by accumulating that which brings only pleasure. "*Nabibhenatarpaniyahamanusyah.*"

(Man is not to be satisfied by riches.)

Human beings search for deeper meaning of life by penetrating the outer layers of existence. Employing research techniques, they look for this meaning and conduct a quest for the soul embedded in the body and the imperishable in transient worldly desires. For this reason, they do not have to seek it elsewhere by repudiating the body and worldly attachments. However, human beings cannot experience life to the fullest by remaining confined entirely within their bodies. They look for eternity. They constantly search for a bridge that would connect fragments of their experience.

Viktor Frankl, the Viennese psychologist, defined a fulfilled life in the following way: We always look for an answer to this ultimate 'why' whenever we engage in any activity, whatever we say, whatever we hope for and whatever we desperately long for. What is the meaning of my life? What is the meaning of my falling in love with someone and of the dreams I see? What is the meaning of all the desires and the forms of detachment that crowd my life? What is the meaning of all the ties that bind me to others? What is the meaning of my salvation or the heaven I crave for? We keep searching for answers to these questions as we go about the business of living our lives. Like Prince Gautam, we are all born into a kingdom we are meant to inherit. Our quest for the meaning of life takes place against the background of this kingdom. Only those who at least glimpse the meaning can find fulfilment. No task appears trivial to them. Everything they do— their pleasure, their sacrifices, their acquisitions and their abdications, their worldly life, and their life in heaven— is blessed with harmony.

Without subjecting life to scrutiny, human beings unquestioningly assign validity and value to practices prevailing in society, if they are backed by scriptural sanction. Over the ages, man's religious outlook has undergone changes under the pressure of his biases and prejudices. In various religions of the world, we find instances of literature being written in defence of such opportunism. In Europe, in the early years of Christianity, leading an austere life was cherished as an ideal. Jesus Christ, the Great Soul, was the embodiment of life lived according to this ideal. Inspired by such maxims, religious leaders of the time openly denigrated kings and landlords who had amassed immeasurable wealth. However, with the passage of time, churches started accumulating wealth and the heads of monasteries became complete strangers to simple living. Spreading spirituality came to be considered a minor activity of the Church, which concentrated on increasing its wealth and power. Churches came to be the owners of large landed estates, and abbots who headed these estates began to lose their progressive outlook. The books written by Saint Francis celebrating the simplicity and austerity of life led by Jesus were rewritten at the instance of the Pope in the 4th century C.E. The belief that Christ had embraced poverty was declared heresy in a decree issued by the Church. The Pope's love for pomp and wealth did not allow him to accept that the founder of his religion was a poor man who remained in poverty all his life.

How can one, standing in the fabulously rich monasteries founded by Shankar in India, say that their founder led a life of poverty? Who will not feel uncomfortable when someone declares in the presence of expensive images of the Buddha and Mahavir in the temples patronized by rich merchants that these two great saints had preached that a simple life devoid of craving should be cherished? If literature is drawn to power, it will suffer the same terrible fate.

Like opium, race and nation could also intoxicate a writer and demand his complete surrender. Using literature to transform a nation into a golden idol, people had then offered it all kinds of oblations. In a particular period in

European history, this was a dominant fashion. German writers were at the forefront of those that used literature to generate a mighty river of nationalism that eventually burst its banks. Nationalist literature and nationalist writers are a German gift to the world. German theologians and philosophers, such as Martin Luther, Fichte, Hegel preached that the conquest of the world is essential for the development of the human soul. A German writer claimed that from the age of Adam, all great men in history bore German blood. The Greek emperor, Alexander, also belonged to the German race. He also presented German as the earliest language of mankind. He expressed the view that in the continents of Asia and Africa there lived German-speaking groups in the past. He was confident that the German race would rule the whole world. During the reign of Hitler, a German author got carried away and declared that the German race was created by Providence as the saviour of humanity. It is therefore the duty of the German race to germanise mankind. Mankind will be saved only if it is placed under the imperial rule of a German monarch. According to this author, this imperial ambition was kindled in the minds of Germans by Martin Luther. German philosopher Leibniz believed that German was the greatest language of the world, and it was the language of heroes. This spirit infected other European countries in a short span of time.

A manifesto signed by 54 French authors expressed the hope that, after the end of the War, France would emerge as the victor. They visualized the whole world assembling under the banner of a triumphant France and prophesied that their nation would emerge as the custodian of mankind. During the Indian subcontinent's struggle for independence, a nationalist tendency contaminated the outlook of the resistors. Fuelled by nationalist sentiments, literature journeyed into the past. And an attempt was made to present the totality of our past as a symbol of our nationhood. In Odisha, Lord Jagannath and Lord Balabhadra were transformed into custodians of Odia national identity. Odias were dressed up as invincible warriors and sent out to conquer heaven and earth. Efforts have been made to prove that ancient sage Vyasadeva and the mediaeval poet Jayadeva belonged to Odisha. Writers who have accepted nationalism as the religion of literature would like to see their own nation ascending the highest throne in the world. The desire for immediate gratification of their wishes drove them towards an obsession with the past. Dragging their predecessors into their own fantasies, they felt that they had achieved their objectives.

In the pre-independence era, nationalism had been worshipped as a deity in India. Now that independence has been attained, which deity would these writers worship?

Who becomes the object of their devotion? The reins of governance have come into our own hands after independence. Now we have become our own masters. In short, we have begun wielding a lot of power. Many did not realise that power is not a source of pleasure, but that it involves great responsibilities. They plunged themselves into the world of politics. Their politics had nothing to do with building human character. Perhaps the independence struggle had left them so worn-out that once they became powerful, they forgot that they had duties to perform. Some writers began entertaining similar ambitions and followed the footsteps of these new political Brahmins. In the past, poets used to lavish praise on the king in his royal court. The king gave them rewards and honours to amuse and divert himself. After independence, something similar happened in our country. Academies were established to bring about an artificial but impressive union between literature and the public sphere. Eminent writers, from different linguistic communities, were nominated to the Rajya Sabha. It may be interesting to examine how their writing changed after they were placed on pedestals. One suspects that they then reined in the living literary movement of their country. In the Romantic era of Indian literature, Rabindranath Tagore provocatively called upon the young and enthusiastic young poets of the new generation to infuse vitality into their half-dead fellow countrymen. Now that the tree which was planted in the Romantic age has started bearing fruit, the half dead of the country have come to dominate the young and the inexperienced. In the first two decades after independence, literature in Odisha survived on political patronage. In this shameful era, to sustain themselves and to achieve recognition, writers had sought the munificence of ministers. In all literary meetings and functions, the glittering crown adorning the head of a politician outshone, and threw into shadow, creative writers.

Many are apprehensive that sources of literary inspiration would dry up without the patronage of people occupying positions of political power. The jubilation of writers knows no bounds if they could be photographed alongside a minister. A professor feels his life is fulfilled if he gets an opportunity to sit beside a minister at a public meeting and exchange a few words with him. When this happens, it is to be expected that the administration or the organisers of the meeting need not feel embarrassed; strangely, the writers themselves do not feel overcome with shame.

In recent times, in Odisha, a couple of writers have appeared on the literary scene, who have sent their roots deep into the political world; literature has become a secondary pursuit for them. They have actively participated in the political process, violated all moral principles, and committed all sorts of immoral deeds. But they lose no opportunity to attend literary meetings. We come across some people who used to consider literature the mission of their lives and politics a minor pursuit. They have now gotten sucked into the vortex of politics and accepted power as an alternative to literature.

This has caused great damage to literature and has diminished our dignity whether we accept it or not. Had we remained committed to literature, we would have devoted our entire energies to pursuing it. But with the vain hope of rising high by clutching the tail of the powerful, we have lost our identity as writers and the opportunity to achieve literary excellence.

These days, literary meetings involve a great deal of pomp and ostentation. But at these, we simply indulge in beating our own drums. Those who pursue political power and enjoy its fruits have not been able to shape the destiny of people nor have they built a better world. For instance, a doctor who enters politics does not become a better doctor nor does he contribute anything meaningful to the practice of medicine. Similarly, writers who enter politics and crave public adulation and must remain content with that. In the *Gita,* it is stated that God appears to a devotee in the form he wishes to see Him in. The form in which God appears to him is determined by the devotee and our desires shape the course of our lives. If a writer longs for power, he turns himself into a servitor on the chariot of politics.

If he wants to make money, he avidly engages in writing textbooks. In doing so, he acquires property, earns fame, occupies important positions, owns impressive houses, but he surrenders his liberty to someone else. One who is a slave of someone else can never create literature in the true sense of the term. Such literature can be written only if one pays undivided attention to the world around him and the deepest commitments embedded in the recesses of his heart. Vinoba Bhave observes that writers today offer worship to Lakshmi, the goddess of wealth and not Saraswati, the goddess of learning. They would be able to exercise an influence on society only if they turn away from Goddess Lakshmi and show devotion to Goddess Saraswati. As they cultivate rich men — blessed by Goddess Lakshmi — they allow themselves to be enslaved by the former.

Modern psychologists are of the view that everyone should devote themselves to doing what they love to do. If one's profession and vocation diverge radically from each other, one's self comes to be fragmented. Writers, who long to participate in power and politics, lead fragmented lives; they also bring misery into the world of literature. Writers who are obsessed with making money find that their creativity has completely dried up.

It is said that Goddess Lakshmi appeared before sage Valmiki and offered him untold riches when he set out on a quest to attain literary creativity. But, as Valmiki wanted to seek the blessings of Saraswati, the goddess of learning, he humbly requested Lakshmi to return to paradise. Though the story is not true, its implicit suggestion reminds the writer of the highest ideals he should cherish. An excellent allegory indicates the conflict between the pursuit of literary and material achievements. When one climbs a mountain, one may find relief under a shady tree during his tiring journey. But if he stops there, he would deprive himself of the opportunity to survey the landscape spreading below from the lofty peak of the mountain. Love for literature is the same as love for life and a sense of responsibility to life represents the highest peak a writer should aspire to reach. Political power, money and adulation are like the cool breeze that tempts a climber to discontinue his journey to the top of the mountain.

Science advances by trying to understand the laws of nature. Scientific discoveries make invention of new machines possible. But we cannot describe a scientist as a mere slave of the laws of nature or a machine. If a scientist unquestioningly reveres the past, he will cease to be a scientist. The scientist must prepare himself to ceaselessly explore new areas of knowledge by refusing to accept the prevailing system as the only possibility. According to the eminent American historian of science Jacob Bronowski, a scientist should keep the banner of revolt against existing conventions and established ways of thought. The same applies to the writer. When the vision of the whole world is clouded by illusions, only writers by engaging in iconoclasm can snap people out of such reverie.

When the whole country indulges in mindless extravagance, writers must have the courage to point out the emptiness underlying pompous boastfulness. Before kowtowing to the dominant conventions of an age, they should learn to be true to the spirit of literature. When falling foul of powerful conventions, one would defy them like Socrates and say, "I shall obey the dictates of God, not yours." The dictates of God here mean one's deepest commitments, one's conscience to which one can offer one's creativity and talent as oblation. In Albert Schweitzer's words, "If you choose the pursuit of philosophy as a way of life, you have to tread a hard and stony path. To be able to negotiate this path successfully, you have to toughen your spine." Pursuit of literature also involves treading a similar path. A writer, too, needs a tough spine.

John F. Kennedy, the former American president had once said that when power makes one behave with arrogance, poetry makes him aware of his limitations. When power makes man's vision shrink, poetry expands his sense of possibilities. What Kennedy says of poetry applies to the whole of literature.

Translated by **Anuja Khatua**

Man at the Centre of the World

Throughout its history, India has never treated all its people as equal members of society. Indian scriptures have not raised questions concerning this issue. Of course, as a token consolation or as a distraction, it has been said that God resides in each person in the form of the soul; but for some reason or the other, this philosophy has been either sidelined or relegated to the background. It is almost as though this sliver of knowledge has been kept hidden in a maze of complex rituals; and consciously kept out of life's daily chores.

A spark lies hidden in an ash heap and is only used to animate philosophical discourses. Wrapped up in an esoteric language, unintelligible to common people, such truths are of no use to anyone. This philosophy has only served to humour those who have wished to live in the illusion of their sanctified existence. An irony down the ages, this role of Indian Philosophy has also remained a shameful obstacle in the path of Indian spirituality. The cunning ones have failed to offer a solution to this problem and have therefore laboured hard to wish it away.

Even now, Indian society does not treat all its members equally. Some clever individuals continue to stage their pantomimes behind the facade of a modern democracy. Even now, there are sages who chant the sacred *stotras* of the Vedas and Upanishads, only to show that they belong to a different class. In real life, they are deeply immersed in empty rituals, merely to keep themselves distanced from "lesser mortals". The Vedantists have transformed themselves into heads of mutts. Attached to their thrones, they look down upon ordinary people with utter disdain. This tendency is also validated by the scriptures.

As long as the world is ruled by these kinds of lies and hypocrisies, by diseased and cunning desires, even God will not have the confidence to come down to the earth. And till then, the custodians of religions would go on duping the world. People wearing colourful robes and looking like saintswill roam around, diverting people's attention, ensuring that they remain lazy and unhealthy. Temples would multiply and a conspiracy to pass off idols as God would gain strength. Religion makes sure that men can never hear the call of the real God who dwells in them waiting to see them shed lethargy.

Religion has cast its net wide through all kinds of ceremonies and tricks. How can the real doors of aspiration open now? It may so happen that, during moments of intense social churning, man will look inwards and find the truth lying within him. Only then would he gain the courage to look outward with love. Having two square meals a day need not be his only preoccupation. These realizations would be possible only when everyone has enough food to eat. This new consciousness can rightly be termed as the second phase of human evolution.

Fulfilling our material needs has become our only preoccupation to the extent of making us paranoic about it. The root cause of this is inadequate provisioning for all members of the society. Those who lack the necessities, are not able to think beyond fulfilling their immediate needs. Those who have more than what they need, remain in a state of perpetual anxiety and aggression lest the deprived ones rise and demolish their happy homes.

As a result, life on both sides looks lustreless and miserable, without any aspiration for attaining higher ideals in life. Nearly all the competitions are here for snatching something from others. Under these conditions, there are limits to what nationalism can achieve. How can you change the world or appeal to emotions while men remain unacceptable to one another, and the current moral standards allow many to be deprived of equal opportunities on the egregious assumption that inequality is a part of natural order?

The history of the modern world reveals that people in countries where basic needs have been fulfilled, are less prone to coveting material needs. In such countries, people aspire for something more than what is needed for basic survival, and qualities like liberalism and tolerance keep improving. In those countries, the belief that there is a world beyond one's own society is common. In old societies, resources were limited and those having access to them had the tendency to dominate others. Fear and superstition ruled over men. People worshipped gods to protect themselves and their privileges. It was the job of the larger mass of people to ensure that the privileges of the affluent remained intact. Economy and politics were structured accordingly.

Meanwhile, the countries which ensured that everyone had access to basic needs also became the cradles of new thoughts. These thoughts and ideas spread all over the world and initiatives were taken to translate them into reality. Accordingly, new global institutions were built. God came closer to the earth, as it were.

Food and work, shelter, and education for all children– these are the most effective ways of making the earth a better place. This is becoming clearer as more people share this vision of a new spiritual order and make all possible efforts to achieve it. These efforts will illustrate the irrelevance of all sectarianism and religious factionalism. Many so-called ideologies would also become irrelevant.

Even the caste system would become irrelevant. If division ceases to exist, caste conflicts would also disappear. Today, one feels respectable only if one shows himself as superior to others. When divisions cease to exist, there would be no need for a false sense of respect. Man's only identity would be that of a human being, known for his abilities and his empathy for others. In the present hierarchical society, there is no opportunity for these qualities to be recognized.

The rot in the caste system runs so deep that even children find themselves divided and clubbed into different categories. This prevents them from growing up into kind and loving human beings. It is as if a conspiracy has been hatched to prevent the country and society from changing for the better. It appears that this brutal system has been so ingrained in us that even after so many years of independence, we are unable to do away with it.

In ancient times, no one possibly imagined that all children of the country would go to schools. When we proudly talk about education in *gurukuls* in ancient India, we never take into consideration, education for all the children— whether there were good number of *gurukuls* for all children or not. Even now, there are zealous people among us who believe that the ancient *gurukul* system can instantly solve all the problems of education. Whether they genuinely believe it or not, they gleefully bring it up every now and then. In reality, they expose their inability to confront the real problems in our education system and try to sidestep them with emotional outpourings.

In this ancient land of Vedantic philosophy, none can deny that God exists in every child. Yet, the babus holding the reins of the system have made different provisions for children of different castes and classes. It is not known at what stage of the Indian social history the Brahmin devised a strategy to turn his child into a priest, and simultaneously condemned the shudra to be skilled only in his caste-occupation. A conspiracy by the privileged ensured that shudras remained in a state of a perpetual servitude. As of now, there is no uniform curriculum for all children at the primary level. As in previous ages, in the present times also most of the people belonging to these classes remain poor unlike those who belong to higher classes. And those differences have been justified in the name of fate. We are asked to believe in the logic that merit resides in wealth or class, in accordance with God's will.

Half the children of this country do not attend any school. Most of them are from the lower, poorer classes. If all the children of this country had the opportunities according to the constitution, no child would have been out of school in the last thirty years. There are great sages and saints in this country, and yet none among them has emphasized this point. They offer discourses on Vedanta and the *Gita,* mostly to elite audiences. Have they decided not to highlight specific aspects of the Vedantic discourse that may not please the privileged?

The children, fortunate enough to be enrolled in schools, do not follow a uniform curriculum. There is discrimination among children belonging to different classes though all educational philosophies and theories pronounce that children should have opportunities according to their aptitude and talent. And yet the managers of our system deliberately go on violating these principles. When a child, at the elementary level, imbibes the nation's spirit, culture, and destiny, she would identify herself with them. Our callous ignorance has led us to place children in different categories. As a result of this discriminatory system, some pursue their studies in comfort with a view to appropriating all benefits, while others have access to such education that would keep them perpetually in inferior vocations in the service of the privileged.

Amidst all these mindless arrangements, spiritual development remains an impossibility. Instead of being drawn to one another, men are being trained to be indifferent the world and be selfish. They are learning to remain indifferent like the sadhus of the past. They are busy pursuing their own happiness and deliverance, even in modern India, as it were. The ancient philosophy that the world is an illusion seems to be asserting itself in its new incarnation.

There are many countries in the world where, despite differences in family incomes, every child is allowed to realize his talent and potential and the entire society feels happy about it. One does not hesitate to acknowledge that real spirituality in all its senses resides in the conscience of those countries. India's children appear to be tied to the destiny of their parents, irrespective of the possibilities in them. As if they get habituated to remain within their limitations.

One fails to understand how India tied even God in the rope of caste. As a result, feelings of empathy and fraternity have been mercilessly confined to narrow spaces. Is there even one village in India where all children can play together at one place completely oblivious of their family circumstances? It appears as if their joy also lies fragmented like their hamlets and castes. And that they would follow a uniform curriculum in one school and that society would take equal care of them, remains even a more distant dream.

The cunning people at the top managed to align their gods with their goals. But how could the gods of the deprived and marginalized people tolerate such discriminations? Why do they fail to confront society with this truth? Perhaps, this kind of thing happens in societies where God is worshipped in the form of multiple deities. In such places, even God must suffer such ignominy.

This has not deterred pundits from making boastful claims of India being the cradle of spirituality. Occasionally, visionaries have protested and propagated new messages, with a call to return to the real truths. But ignorant followers have turned them into gods. Thus, Gautam Buddha was turned into God. Even Mahatma Gandhi, whom many of us have seen in our own eyes, has been elevated into a deity in the temple.

Even kings have roped in God in their campaigns for conquering territories. In the process they have cunningly deluded people. Even today, there are crazy fanatics, who are proud of their incendiary abilities. They stupidly believe in the victory of their God over the other God. If man really seeks God and truth, he will easily realize whether there are different Gods for every religion or some men in their utter arrogance have kept God captive within their narrow confines. The long hand of the so-called religious preceptors or communal leaders can be seen in all the religious wars and conflicts that the world has witnessed. The same hands are busy keeping quite many people addicted to the opium of religion even in this age. It is not always true that modernity in an outer sense is positively correlated with cognitive maturity. One cannot claim that hate has declined in the modern world. On the other hand, man would have possibly done away with the old orthodoxies if he had become aware of the real challenges facing him. He would have rediscovered God through a new relationship.

Walking towards God means ascending the steps of one's potentiality and aspirations. Every man is born into a family or community. Outwardly the family and community belong to a religion. Thus, every man is also born into a religion. With age, man grows in intelligence, experience and understanding. As he climbs up higher, he sees more. The circles of his acquaintances also grow. The heart goes on expanding. Realizing in the natural course that the old idols would no longer be adequate, man should be able to scale greater heights. All the achievements and inheritance of the entire world are within the grasp of all men now. This should take them to an unprecedented level of consciousness and solidarity. Consequently, men would come closer to another, the outward casing would fall, all the artificialities and divisive tendencies would disappear. A new type of foundation would get built for tomorrow's world. In such a world different opinions and ideas would be mutually complementary. Science would aid religion in different ways so that it is possible for men to receive the signal of a new spirituality from within themselves. This would infect the outer world in an auspicious way.

But this has not happened since a hard sectarian vision has got man's conscience in its grip. It appears, the education system of the world has wrongly taught men to remain prisoners of their grooves. The people who treat the grooves as God are destined to be miserably hapless, however powerful they may look. From this growing sense of defeat, they get an excuse to be aggressively individualistic. The world's politics is being conducted with wicked intelligence; affluence makes indulgence in luxuries possible; and yet man is unable to return home. The grooves may have their fatal attraction, but it has not been possible to restore faith in the mind of the sick. Soothsayers have started sounding an alarm that this world would not last long. It has been filled up with a variety of protests and agitations. Many people are taking the help of opium to induce sleep to avoid experiencing the chaos.

The world would change when man returns to man, when men seek out and return to one another the world would change. In today's world men are searching for everything other than men. They are after wealth, fame, power and positions. They are competing with one another to prove their superiority in wealth and power. As far as the heart is concerned, they have at the most come up to the level of their families, country, caste, or religion.

Laying a strong foundation for men would be the primary task of religion, knowledge, and science. There always have been a plethora of differences between men, in both inward and outward senses. There are differences in nature. But all these differences will have to be evaluated against the fundamental similarities. This will be possible if men, gurus, and leaders stop showing their one-up-man-ship over men and God.

Millions of people cry over their destiny, pleading to God through devotional songs for early release from the ephemeral world. Another group of people try to ingratiate themselves to God by building temples and with holy offerings, proudly riding over men as if they were horses, and giving credit to God for their fortune. What kind of world is it? What kind of divinity God is? That the world finds itself in such a state is not really the fault of God. In fact, this is the handiwork of the men who have lost their conscience.

The old gurus have outlived their utility. May God bless those who worship God in solitary caves. But the world will not change through them. He, who stays in the world with God as company, not ask anything for himself, not even seeking paradise, and works for the world, fighting against orthodoxies, he only can perform the task and make a new world possible. There would be no need for such a man to break any temple or mosque, nor join any race for political power. But, when such men come together, live mutually rewarding lives without compromise and refuse to bow their heads before the wicked, this would cause a massive stir. Those men will be the leaders, they will play both the roles, that of the guru and the follower. They will not form any sect but will create a new faith. This will give them abundant joy. This is no simple task.

Translated by **Aurobindo Behera**
An excerpt from 'Saba Mulare Manisha'
(The Man is Root at Everything)

A Moment of Decision

In 1942, the British government suffered defeat after defeat at the hands of the Japanese army in the battlefields of Asia. Japanese war planes occasionally bombed the eastern part of India. Once the Japanese bombed and sank a few Allied warships off the Odisha coast. The wounded soldiers were brought over to Cuttack. Plans were drawn to put them up in the hostels of Ravenshaw College and we were asked to vacate our rooms immediately. The political atmosphere in India became charged as the final battle for independence seemed imminent.

When I came back to the college hostel after the summer holidays, I was allotted a single room upstairs for I had done well in the first-year degree examination. On the 9th of August, Mahatma Gandhi called upon the British to quit India. The Government arrested Gandhi and all other leaders in the country. For a couple of days after this, I was too restless to concentrate on anything. I shut myself up in my room. It was as if the moment had arrived to take a crucial decision not only for the whole country but also for myself.

I did not attend classes during this period. One morning, I walked all the way to my brother's residence in Bamphi Sahi. I confessed to him that my heart was no longer in my studies and that I wanted to join the freedom struggle. I was apprehensive that, on hearing this, he would scold me. Since my childhood he had pinned very high hopes on me, and was extremely fond of me. He used to tell everyone that, when I grew older, I would become an ICS officer. Was not I dashing all his fondest dreams? But, most unexpectedly, he buttressed my sagging resolve. He said to me, "Even I feel like giving up my government job and throwing myself into Gandhi's movement at a time like this. But I have so many family responsibilities to shoulder, which cannot be overlooked. But your case is different. If you really want to take part in the struggle, do so by all means. However, I must say that you should not give in to a momentary impulse and go to jail. When the excitement of the moment has passed, you would regret your mistake. Maybe, you would go so far as to want to apologise to the government to get out of jail. This will be a terrible thing to happen and, for the rest of your life, you will feel guilty." He advised me to go to our village. Some agitational activities would be undertaken there under Gouribhai's leadership, and I would be able to take part in these. Participation in the struggle would give me a chance to find out if I had chosen the right path. I could stay with the movement and go to jail, if I felt like it. Alternatively, I could withdraw from the struggle and resume my studies. He said all this very calmly.

His words made me happy, and I came back to the hostel. A lot of confusion within me had been dispelled and I was now ready to arrive at a decision. It had seemed as if someone's blessings had burnt away a lot of my doubts and made me feel much lighter. By this time, the August revolution had set the country on fire, as it were.

The big leaders of the Congress party in Odisha had all been sent to jail. Our college had been placed under strict police surveillance to prevent anyone from instigating the students. The superintendents of our hostel behaved as if they wholeheartedly supported the government's activities. They were not so much opposed to the August Revolution, as they feared losing their jobs. At night I said nothing about my decision to any of my friends in the hostel. I got up early in the morning, took my bath and hung my wet lungi to dry on the door and set off. At least for a day or two, no one would suspect that I was absent. The lungi drying on the door would keep people from finding out if there was someone inside. I took care not to lock the door.

I came to the canal embankment, which lay on the southern side of the college, and walked along it towards Nuabazar. From there, people travelled to Jagatsinghpur by boats pulled by hand. For going to my village, I had to travel in one of these up to Balia. The fare was four annas. The boat would leave Nuabazar at about nine or ten in the morning and reach Balia around four in the afternoon. On the way, one sometimes changed boats at Kaijanga. My village Bagalpur was two kilometers from Balia. It was getting dark by the time I reached home. I explained to my family members that I had come home because the college had been closed on account of the nationalist agitation. Of course, that was the case. On being asked if I had informed my elder brother, I said that I had done so. Gouribhai was away from the village at the time. Two days later, he came from Cuttack, travelling by foot along a winding path. He was accompanied by Gobind Chandra Mohanty, who belonged to Satpura, a neighbouring village. Gouribhai's right hand was deformed from birth. He was popularly known as khandi Gourang Das. There was always the danger of being caught, so they travelled only at night, and during day time hid themselves in someone's house.

When they arrived in the village, I went to them to enquire about the future course of the struggle. They told us that at the Congress Convention Gandhi's message was 'do or die.' Every Indian should act according to the dictates of his own conscience and fight British rule. Many leaders in Orissa and the rest of the country had been imprisoned. Many had gone underground. The latter would now carry on the struggle. Surendra Nath Dwivedi was hiding in Cuttack. He would be the link between Orissa and the world outside, and all of us would get united and act as a single group. As a result of restrictions imposed by the government, newspapers would not carry news about what was happening all over the country, which was in the grip of the August Revolution. Therefore, news had to flow from one province to the other through informal channels. All of us should remain in touch with Dwivedi living in Cuttack, and Bagalpur would function as the centre for all villages nearby. News and directions would be sent from Cuttack. Pamphlets carrying these would be printed in Bagalpur, which would then be distributed through a network operating with extreme secrecy.

I was entrusted with the task of getting the pamphlets printed. There was a litho machine in the village minor school, which was chiefly used to print question papers. We spoke to the headmaster of this school and it was decided that we would use this machine. Stencil sheets, paper, and printer's ink would be sent from Cuttack by Dwivedi. Precautions would be taken to ensure that nobody knew that pamphlets were being printed at the school. Not even the students or the hostel boarders should get an inkling. So, all the work had to be done at night. Every night after dinner I would come to the school, carrying a hurricane lamp. It was the month of August. The village path was deep in mud in places. As I had to plod through sticky mud, I carried a bamboo staff. By the time I would reach the school, most of the boarders would be asleep or would be going to bed. The headmaster would be waiting for me in the office room. He would hand me the key and go home. I would set to work after this. A messenger would bring news from Cuttack. I would add to this some of my own writings. Now and then I would write a fiery poem calling upon people to fight the British. It would be midnight before the day's work was done. Everything was done in such secrecy so that even the teachers could suspect nothing.

The village chowkidar, Keshab, came to the school veranda after making a few rounds at night and slept there. The moment he arrived, I would stop all work, close the door behind me, come out and spend five to ten minutes gossiping with him. He would tell me what was going on at the police station. Those days, the police station was in Gobindpur, which stood on the bank of the river Debi. Keshab thought that I was studying or writing something in the office room. He would tell me, "Baboo, do your work. Do not let anything scare you. I am sleeping on the veranda." The very thought that I was writing and printing pamphlets with the aim of driving the British out of India, while their agent slept on the veranda outside, struck me as extremely funny. After my work for the night was finished, I would carefully burn the ink-stained stencil paper. I would clean the machine and neatly sort out the papers. Having done this, I would go to sleep. My younger brother, Deba, was a student of class seven at this school at the time. He was staying in the hostel. He would leave some space on his rush-mat for me to sleep on. I would lie down beside him and get up before other children left their beds. I would finish my ablutions by the river, take my bath, come back to the school, and return the keys to the headmaster. Then I would go back home, carrying the hurricane lamp and the bamboo staff. My younger brother was under the impression that I did some work at night and went to sleep beside him after it was over. Beyond this he knew nothing. Besides, he was too young to go deeper into the matter.

Translated by **Jatindra Kumar Nayak**
An excerpt from 'Mitrasya Chakshusa'
(Through the eyes of a friend)
Cuttack: S.B. Publications, 1998

About the Translators

Ananta Kumar Giri is a Professor at the Madras Institute of Development Studies, Chennai. He has written, edited, and translated more than seventy books in Odia and English.

Anjali Sahoo teaches English at Panchayat Degree College, Bargarh, Odisha

Anuja Khatua teaches English at Government Polytechnic, Puri in Odisha. Her English translation of Nanda Kishore Bal's novel, Kanakalata was published in 2015 by Rupantar and GopinathMohanty's Apahancha was published by Sahitya Akademi, New Delhi in 2021.

Ashim Sabat is an alumnus of Regional Engineering College (NIT-Rourkela), where he also received a postgraduate degree in Metallurgical Engineering. Presently he is serving as a General Manager in Rourkela Steel Plant

Aurobindo Behera is a former civil servant. He is a columnist and translator.

Bijaya Kumar Nanda is a bilingual writer, essayist, critic, translator, editor, and biographer. He taught English literature at several government colleges in Odisha.

Birendra Kumar Nayak is a former Professor of Mathematics (Utkal University), an author and critic. He is the editor of The Tribal Tribune, an e-magazine which publishes research related to tribal communities in India.

Biswajit Apat is a Post-Doctoral Fellow at the National Institute of Science Education and Research, Bhubaneswar. His research focuses on issues concerning administration and equity in school systems.

Braja Mohan Mishra is a translator and critic. He has translated Chittaranjan Das' biography of Nabakrushna Choudhury: Eka Jibani. It was published by National Book Trust, New Delhi.

Dinesh Prasad Pattanayak is a former Head of the Department of English, Ravenshaw College.

Guru Charan Beherais a former Professor of English, Banaras Hindu University, Varanasi. He has publishedfour books of criticism in English and Odia, and around fifty research papers in national and international journals.

Janmejay Dwivedi is a retired Reader in English and an author.

Jayanta Biswal retired as principal of a government college in Odisha. He is an author, columnist, and translator. He is one of the founding members of Nabapallab, Bhubaneswar.

Kalidas Misra is a former professor at the PG Department of English Literature, Sambalpur University. He was part of the Orissa Research Project of the German Research Council, Heidelburg.

Rabindra Kumar Swain is a poet, translator, editor, and critic. His translations from Odia into English include The

Cemetery Flower and Other Stories by Sachi Routray, Temporary Address and Other Stories by Ramachandra Behera.

Sangram Jena is a poet and award-winning translator. He has published more than 30 books. At present he is the Vice –President, Odisha Sahitya Academy.

Santosh Kumar Mishra is an author, translator, and editor. Currently he is engaged in translation and creative works for children.

Satyananda Swain is a retired Reader in English. His English translation of Stuti Chintamani of Bhima Bhoi (Gems of Soulful Prayer) has been published by NBT.

Urmishree Bedamatta teaches in the Department of English at Ravenshaw University. Currently, she is the Director of the Centre for Digital Humanities at the university.

Black Eagle Books

www.blackeaglebooks.org
info@blackeaglebooks.org

Black Eagle Books, an independent publisher, was founded as a nonprofit organization in April, 2019. It is our mission to connect and engage the Indian diaspora and the world at large with the best of works of world literature published on a collaborative platform, with special emphasis on foregrounding Contemporary Classics and New Writing.

www.ingramcontent.com/pod-product-compliance
Lightning Source LLC
Chambersburg PA
CBHW020152120726
47903CB00007B/2526
* 9 7 8 1 6 4 5 6 0 5 4 1 6 *